EXPLORING SCOTLAND'S HERITAGE

£3.50

EXPLORING SCOTLAND'S HERITAGE
ARGYLL AND THE WESTERN ISLES

Graham Ritchie and Mary Harman

The Royal Commission
on the Ancient and Historical Monuments
of Scotland

Edinburgh
Her Majesty's Stationery Office

Royal Commission on the Ancient and Historical Monuments of Scotland
54 Melville Street, Edinburgh EH3 7HF (031-225 5994)

The Commission, which was established in 1908, is responsible for compiling a national record of archaeological sites and historic buildings of all types and periods. The Commission makes this record available both through its publications (details of which can be obtained from the above address) and through the maintenance of a central archive of information, known as the National Monuments Record of Scotland, which contains an extensive collection of pictorial and documentary material relating to Scotland's ancient monuments and historic buildings and is open daily for public reference at 6-7 Coates Place, Edinburgh EH3 7AA.

Other titles in the series

Lothian and the Borders
Orkney and Shetland
The Clyde Estuary and Central Region
Dumfries and Galloway
The Highlands
Grampian
Fife and Tayside

ISBN 0 11 492429 5

CONTENTS

FOREWORD

Twentieth century Scotland has a heritage of human endeavour stretching back some nine thousand years, and a wide range of man-made monuments survives as proof of that endeavour. The rugged character of much of the Scottish landscape has helped to preserve many antiquities which elsewhere have vanished beneath modern development or intensive deep ploughing, though with some 3850 km of coastline round mainland alone there has also been an immeasurable loss of archaeological sites as a result of marine erosion. Above all, perhaps, the preservation of such a wide range of monuments should be credited to Scotland's abundant reserves of good building stone, allowing not only the creation of extraordinarily enduring prehistoric houses and tombs but also the development of such remarkable Scottish specialities as the medieval tower-house and the iron-age broch. This volume is one of a series of eight handbooks which have been designed to provide up-to-date and authoritative introductions to the rich archaeological heritage of the various regions of Scotland, highlighting the most interesting and best preserved of the surviving monuments and setting them in their original social context. The time-scale is the widest possible, from relics of World War II or the legacy of 19th century industrial booms back through history and prehistory to the earliest pioneer days of human settlement, but the emphasis varies from region to region, matching the particular directions in which each has developed. Some monuments are still functioning (lighthouses for instance), others are still occupied as homes, and many have been taken into the care of the State or the National Trust for Scotland, but each has been chosen as specially deserving a visit.

Thanks to the recent growth of popular interest in these topics, there is an increasing demand for knowledge to be presented in a readily digestible form and at a moderate price. In sponsoring this series, therefore, the Royal Commission on the Ancient and Historical Monuments of Scotland broadens the range of its publications with the aim of making authentic information about the man-made heritage available to as wide an audience as possible.

Graham Ritchie and Mary Harman have combined their extensive knowledge of Argyll and the Western Isles to write this volume. Graham Ritchie is an Investigator with the Royal Commission on the Ancient and Historical Monuments of Scotland and has spent the last twenty-four years recording and excavating monuments in Argyll, while Mary Harman is a freelance archaeologist and anatomist, who has worked on Lewis and extensively on St Kilda and consequently has an intimate knowledge of the Western Isles.

Monuments have been grouped according to their character and date and, although only the finest, most interesting or best preserved have been described in detail, attention has also been drawn to other sites worth visiting in the vicinity. Each section has its own explanatory introduction, beginning with the most recent monuments and gradually retreating in time back to the earliest traces of prehistoric man.

Each major monument is numbered and identified by its district so that it may easily be located on the end-map, but it is recommended that the visitor should also use the relevant 1:50,000 maps published by the Ordnance Survey as its Landranger Series, particularly for the more remote sites. Sheet nos 8, 13, 14, 18, 22 and 31 cover the Outer Hebrides, while Skye and Lochaber require sheet nos 23, 32, 33, 39, 40, 41, 47 and 49. The islands of Coll and Tiree are on sheet no. 46, Mull on nos 47, 48 and 49, and Islay and Jura on nos 60 and 61. The rest of Argyll and Bute from Oban to the Mull of Kintyre is covered by sheet nos 50, 55, 56, 62, 63 and 68. The National Grid Reference for each site is provided (eg NN 132276) as well as local directions at the head of each entry.

An asterisk indicates that the site is subject to restricted hours of opening; unless attributed to Historic Buildings and Monuments, Scottish Development Department (HBM, SDD) or the National Trust for Scotland (NTS), the visitor should assume the monument to be in private ownership and should seek permission locally to view it. It is of course vital that visitors to any monument should observe the country code and take special care to fasten gates. Where a church is locked, it is often possible to obtain the key from the local manse, post office or general store.

We have made an attempt to estimate how accessible each monument may be for disabled visitors, indicated at the head of each entry by a wheelchair logo and a number: 1=easy access for all visitors, including those in wheelchairs; 2=reasonable access for pedestrians but restricted access for wheelchairs; 3=restricted access for all disabled but a good view from the road or parking area; 4=access for the able-bodied only.

Many of the sites mentioned in this handbook are held in trust for the nation by the Secretary of State for Scotland and cared for on his behalf by Historic Buildings and Monuments, Scottish Development Department. Further information about these monuments, including details of guidebooks to individual properties, can be obtained from Historic Buildings and Monuments, PO Box 157, Edinburgh EH3 5DX. Information about properties in the care of the National Trust for Scotland can be obtained from the National Trust for Scotland, 5 Charlotte Square, Edinburgh EH2 4DU. The abbreviation RMS refers to the Royal Museum of Scotland, Queen Street, Edinburgh, whose collections include important material from Argyll and the Western Isles.

ANNA RITCHIE
Series Editor

ACKNOWLEDGMENTS

The Royal Commission's Inventories of the ancient and historical monuments of Argyll and of Skye and the Outer Isles have formed the basis for many entries, and thus the preparation of this volume would not have been possible without the work of many colleagues. Two Secretaries to the Commission, Dr K A Steer and Mr J G Dunbar, have elucidated many aspects of West Highland monumental sculpture and medieval architecture respectively; colleagues in the archaeological and architectural sections, particularly Mr I Fisher, Mr A MacLaren, Mr G S Maxwell, Mr G P Stell and Mr J B Stevenson, have advised in several ways, and in many cases their primary research is summarised here. Mr G D Hay and Mr Stell made freely available the fruits of their research on industrial and historical topics in advance of publication. The achievements of our photographic colleagues, under Mr G B Quick, both in the field and in the studio, are gratefully acknowledged. Although the work of the drawing office is less fully represented in this volume, the clarification of the different periods of a complex building, or the working out of the pattern on a carved stone has depended on their skills and patience; we are thus grateful to our colleagues under Mr I G Scott and Mr S Scott for their assistance in the field and in the office. We are indebted to Mr I G Parker for the maps and for his work on some of the line drawings.

We are indebted to Mr J G Dunbar for many helpful comments on the text.

Under Miss C H Cruft, the National Monuments Record of Scotland has been of great help in providing information about buildings in particular and in tracking down suitable photographs or plans. Miss M I E Steel gave unstintingly of her time in many ways and assisted Miss Harman during fieldwork in Skye and the Outer Isles. Mr Peter Moore kindly commented on those entries for Skye and the Outer Isles. The assistance of Mrs E Glass who took an untidy manuscript and typed it to an impeccable state is gratefully acknowledged, and we are very grateful to Mr I F C Fleming for checking the National Grid references. We are particularly grateful to Dr A Ritchie, the series editor, for her assistance and support throughout the preparation of this volume.

The majority of the photographs are the work of the Commission's Photographic Department or are from the archives of the National Monuments Record of Scotland, and these are Crown Copyright, Royal Commission on the Ancient and Historical Monuments of Scotland. Several photographs were provided by the authors.

We are gratefully indebted to the following institutions and individuals for permission to publish photographs: Scottish Development Department, Historic Buildings and Monuments (Crown Copyright: pp. 31, 44, 74, 75, 80, 86, 117, 119, 124, 127, 130, 137, 139, 140, 142, 145, 150); National Trust for Scotland (pp. 36, 39); Aerofilms (p. 47, opp. p. 49); Campbeltown Library and Museum (p. 60); Mr M Brooks (p. 146); Mrs B Naggar (p. 128); Mr I G Scott (p. 146); Professor D Harding (p. 129); Mrs U V Betts (opp. p. 114); Dr D J Breeze (opp. p. 114); Mr M Gibb (p. 66).

INTRODUCTION

The scenic interplay between the sea and the mountains of the Western Highlands and Islands of Scotland has surely impressed invaders and visitors since early times. The Atlantic coast has been open to seaborne trade and settlement from the beginnings of prehistory. In later times the waters of the North Channel were little barrier to the Scots from Ulster who formed the kingdom of Dalriada in Argyll from about AD 500; in the 14th and 15th centuries the Sea of the Hebrides linked the various territories under the sway of the Lords of the Isles.

For most modern visitors to Argyll and the islands, however, the sea is a barrier, with long lochs necessitating detours round the shore, or straits which must be crossed by ferry. For those who have the sea as their highway the greater part of this area is readily accessible, by navigating round islands and sailing up the sea-lochs, many of which penetrate far inland. Before the building of a road network in the 18th century, the mountainous ridge of the western spine of the Scottish mainland cut off the Atlantic coast from all but the most intrepid travellers or determined armies.

James Watt who came to the Highlands in 1776 in order to report on the possibility of a canal through the Great Glen provided an excellent thumb-nail sketch of the land and its economy. He wrote (with the spelling slightly modernised):

"The Highland mountains, which commence at the Firth of Clyde, extend upon the west side of the country to the northernmost parts of Scotland; in general they begin close at the sea shore; they are intersected by deep but narrow vallies; the quantity of arable land is exceeding small, and its produce greatly lessened by the prodigious rains that fall upon that coast.

The tops of the mountains are craggy, and their sides are steep, but they produce a grass very proper for breeding small black cattle, and in some place for feeding sheep.

The sea coast is exceedingly rugged and rocky, and abounds with great inlets, which are excellent harbours. It is sheltered by many islands, which like the main land, are generally mountainous and rocky, but rather more fertile.

The salt water lochs or arms of the sea, are nurseries for fish, of which many kinds are found in plenty in the seas upon these coasts. The herrings, the cod, and ling, are those which are taken in greatest quantities, and exported to foreign parts; but there are other species, which may perhaps become subjects of trade.

The shores produce in abundance the *Alga Marina,* or seaweed, which being burnt, makes the alkaline salt called kelp. The quantities of the commodity made and consumed of late years are immense, and the rents paid for the kelp of some shores, have borne a great proportion to that of the land they surrounded.

There are in many parts of the country considerable coppice woods of oak and other timbers. The oak woods have been greatly hurt by the destructive practice of cutting them for their bark, the timber being often left to rot upon the spot."

The underlying rock has been subject to many changes in its history, being heated and folded and faulted, and it is this that is in part responsible for the pattern of long north-east south-west glens and lochs, with ridges of hills between. Mull and much of Skye and the Small Isles are of volcanic origin, and the Outer Hebrides, Coll and Tiree are of gneiss, the oldest rock in the British Isles. The whole area has been subject to glaciation which has emphasized some features, deepening some of the valleys into fjords, and scouring the rocks of the Outer Isles. Many of the soils which have developed are acid and large tracts of land are covered by acid peat bogs, but some parts are more suited to agriculture; Islay has areas of boulder clay, limestone and raised beach; Colonsay, Oronsay and Tiree also have raised beaches and Eigg, Muck and Canna have fertile soils derived from lava, similar to those found in parts of Mull. In Sleat and Broadford on Skye, and parts of Raasay, there are good agricultural areas on limestone. Much of the best agricultural land in the Outer Hebrides and parts of the Inner Hebrides, however, is on the *machair*, an alkaline deposit of shell sand, which has accumulated on the western side of south Harris, the Uists and Barra, and also in parts of Lewis, Tiree and Islay, as well as Colonsay and Oronsay. This is especially productive where it overlies the acid peat and the two can be mingled, but the sand alone, particularly when enriched with decaying seaweed, can yield relatively good crops, though wind erosion is a perennial threat once the fragile turf is broken.

About nine thousand years ago when man first began to explore the shoreline, the lochs and the forests of the west of Scotland, the agricultural potential of the land was not his interest. At this time the climate was becoming a little warmer than formerly, and hunting areas could profitably be extended to the north and west. Short hunting forays and fishing expeditions gave way to seasonal camping trips, and gradually the west of Scotland was permanently settled for the first time. The skills of these folk lay in their use of the natural resources of the land and sea, and in the exploitation of the rich harvests at different seasons of the year. They have left few permanent traces for us to see today, but on Oronsay there are several large mounds made up of discarded shells, especially limpets, and layers of blown sand. Radiocarbon dates show that the occupation here was underway by about the middle of the 5th millennium BC; the mounds are impressive, that at Caisteal nan Gillean for example (NR 358879) being over 30 m in diameter and 3.5 m in height. The objects found in the course of excavations show that limpets were not the only item on the menu, and that fishing was also important with crab and birds supplementing the diet. Perhaps at other seasons deer and seal-hunting were major aspects of the economy. Scatters of the tiny flints that the hunters set into hafts to form knives and hunting-blades also show the main areas of settlement; often an attractive bay as at Campbeltown or Oban formed the focus for occupation. In other areas, such as Rum, exploitation of the local stone for tool-making led to early settlement.

The arrival of people who had a wide variety of new skills gradually altered the subsistence pattern of western Scotland from about 4000 BC; knowledge of farming practices, stock-rearing and the growing of cereal crops introduced a way of life that remained unchanged until industrial times. Most of the monuments of this period that one can see today are the massive burial places of these neolithic farmers, with cairns covering the chambers that were used as burial vaults over many hundreds of years. The stones employed in the construction of the chambers are in some cases very large and, together with the size of the cairns, show that the work must have involved a considerable degree of communal organisation. The tombs, quite apart from their practical and religious functions in the disposal of the dead from at least one part of society, may also have provided symbols of the permanence of a community; even if the farmers moved from one part of the area to another as the fields became exhausted, their massive cairns would remain symbols of territoriality. Although several of the tombs of Argyll have been examined in recent years, in none have the deposits survived as completely as those at Isbister, in South Ronaldsay, Orkney, where the discovery of large numbers of the talons of sea-eagles may give us the totem or emblem of the builders and users of the tomb.

One of the most important tools of the farming communities was the stone axe; skilfully hafted in a wooden handle, this made an efficient implement for land clearance and for shaping timbers for building. Axe-heads were widely traded at this time, and many examples of a distinctive stone from Co Antrim in N Ireland have been found in the west of Scotland. Local stone was also employed for tools, as was beach-pebble flint. A remarkable recent discovery at Shulishader, Lewis, was a stone axe-head still with its haft of hawthorn wood, preserved because it had been sealed by moist peat. Five stone axe-heads found together in Loch Airigh na Ceardaich, Balallan, Lewis, include two axes which may be of a Perthshire stone.

By the middle of the third millennium BC the western coast of Scotland again saw maritime contacts that were eventually to lead to a knowledge of metalwork in the area. These are indicated by the discovery of a distinctive type of pottery—Beaker ware. Quantities of such pottery have been found associated with small stone houses at Northton, in Harris, and in several less-well defined settlements in the sand dunes of Uist, Coll and Ardnamurchan. The pottery styles are very similar to those from other parts of Britain and indeed

the continent, but archaeologists are today less inclined to see large-scale invasion by 'Beaker Folk' than to see the introduction of new ideas and fashions to the existing population. In the west of Scotland, however, it does seem likely that a new influx of people was also involved, perhaps into areas sparsely populated earlier. Beaker ware is also found in a new form of burial ritual, deposition of a single body in a small stone coffin or cist (the Scottish word for chest). One of the rare examples of a burial associated with metal objects was found at Salen in Mull in 1882; here the interment was accompanied by a Beaker, two flint flakes and fragments of copper, indicative perhaps of one of Scotland's earliest metal-using communities.

From this period there are no standing settlements to visit, and the burial places of the metal ages are rarely exciting to see except during excavation. On such a site the piles of boulders covering a cist merely serve to stress the great effort and respect involved in their construction. The cairns of the Kilmartin valley provide a dramatic illustration of the potential of such sites after excavation; sadly, however, the early date of their investigation means that some information has undoubtedly been lost. From the cairns there is a wide range of neolithic and bronze-age pottery, including Beaker ware, and a style of later pottery frequently found in bronze-age cists known as Food Vessels—a highly decorated series of bowls and vases. A knowledge of metallurgy is shown by the carvings of bronze axes on the slabs of cists at Nether Largie and Ri Cruin (nos 72-73).

The many impressive standing stones of the west have, since the 18th century, intrigued travellers, who marvelled at the skill of the folk who set them up and at their survival over the centuries. Martin Martin, who in 1697 wrote about the island of St Kilda, described the great stones of Callanish, though not by name, in 1703 in his Description of the Western Isles. Callanish is one of the most spectacular prehistoric sites in Britain; clearance of about 1.5 m of peat from all over the site in 1857 showed the full size and extent of the stones for the first time for three millennia, but it was completed without any of the antiquaries of the day being present. Callanish has, like Stonehenge and Skara Brae, caught popular imagination, but unlike Stonehenge, the visitor to Callanish will be able to ponder the meaning of the stones in comparative calm. There is no reason to doubt that the circle could have been erected around 3000 BC, for radiocarbon dates of this order come from an Orcadian stone circle which is comparable, though less complex; the little chambered tomb at the centre of Callanish is likely to be an addition to the existing circle. Standing stones, stone circles and rock carvings evoke many rituals that we no longer understand; social and religious obligations are difficult to evaluate in prehistoric societies, but they would probably have been potent factors in the way of life of the third and second millennia BC.

The stone circles and settings of Britain may have been set up with the use of a standard unit of measurement, which has been identified by Professor A Thom as the megalithic yard (0.829 m); Thom has also examined one aspect of megalithic architecture that has long puzzled archaeologists: the fact that many 'circles' were neither circular nor regular. He identified groups of standing stones which form egg-shapes and ellipses that could have been laid out using mathematical skills and the megalithic yard. While his theories have not been unchallenged, there is no doubt that they offer a helpful interpretation of features that are otherwise not possible to explain. That the sun and the moon played some part in the religious cosmology of early man is not surprising; a clear and predetermined interest in celestial events may be illustrated at the chambered tomb of Maes Howe, in Orkney, where the rays of the mid-winter setting sun light up the rear wall of the tomb along the narrow passage. It is possible to imagine a line between a single standing stone, a natural point on the horizon (perhaps a notch between two folds in the hills) and the sun or the

moon; the conjunction of these three elements recurs in more or less regular fashion, and such alignments could have been used in a variety of calendrical calculations. But such an interpretation depends not least on the choice of a single marker out of what is often a wide and jagged horizon, and it is also out of keeping with what we understand, however imperfectly, of the nature of society at this time.

The fortifications of the later first millennium BC and the early centuries AD show a more turbulent society with tribal strongholds demanding the constructional effort that earlier went into the piling up of cairns and the erection of stone circles. Prestige may have played a part too in the building of timber-laced hillforts, brochs and duns that were the centres of power of local chieftains. We assume that these folk spoke a Celtic language and were part of a society that may be compared with those described by Caesar and Tacitus. The workers in metal would have been held in high esteem, fashioning not only the weapons for the warriors but also ornaments and jewellery for the chief and his lady.

The west of Scotland probably remained unconcerned by the Roman occupations of parts of the south and east of the country, although maritime activity must have increased, not only with the Roman circumnavigation of the north but also with trade. From Dun Fiadhairt, Skye (no. 62), excavation uncovered a terracotta model of a bale of hides or fleeces, which is certainly a Roman piece, and a few Roman coins and other objects have been found elsewhere, including for example fragments of Roman glass and pottery vessels from Dun Mor, Vaul, Tiree (no. 64). From the early first millennium AD we have some knowledge of the tribal names of the peoples of the west of Scotland: the *Epidii* in Kintyre and the *Creones* between Ardnamurchan and Skye for example. In the centuries before AD 500 contact and settlement from Ulster to Argyll by the *Scotti* established a *Scottic* kingdom known as Dalriada; one of the important centres at this time was Dunadd (no. 54). Excavations at Dunollie (no. 23) show that this naturally impressive rock summit was also occupied at this time; the artefacts uncovered included distinctive imported pottery, bone combs and pins, and moulds for metal working. The radiocarbon analyses indicate a date in the second half of the 7th and the first half of the 8th centuries, corresponding well to the mention in the Irish Annals of the capture and burning of a fort there in 698.

To the north of Dalriada (and Ardnamurchan is usually taken as the northern boundary) lay territories controlled probably by the Picts. The Pictish kingdom was the result of the political fusion of several eastern and north-eastern tribes with the centre of power at this period at the northern end of the Great Glen. It is debatable how strong their control can have been in the islands or along the broken western mainland, but there are several of the distinctive carved symbol stones erected by the Picts including that at Tote, on Skye (no. 52).

The introduction of Christianity to the west of Scotland following the foundation of a monastery on Iona by Columba about 563 increased the status of Dalriada, for it was from here that the new religion was taken to the Picts. For three centuries Iona was at the hub of religious and to some extent political influence in north and west Scotland. Relations between the Scots and the Picts were at times stormy— the Picts captured Dunadd in 736 for example and in 768 the Scots were fighting on Pictish soil in the province of Fortriu. The ruling families of the two kingdoms intermarried, and in about 843 Kenneth mac Alpin, king of Dalriada, became also king of the Picts, partly through his mother's line and perhaps partly by battle. The west lost much of its political importance, for the centre of power of the united kingdom was to be at Scone, in Perthshire, and in 849 Dunkeld succeeded Iona as the centre of ecclesiastical authority.

By the 9th century, however, a new power was taking control of much of the northern and Atlantic seaboard of Scotland—the Vikings. Part of the reason for the later importance of the west to the Norsemen was its position on the route between Norway and the Norse trading centre of Dublin but, although Norse graves and coin hoards have been found, there is little archaeological evidence of extensive settlement. Norse houses have been found, but none can be seen today. There are also very few grave-slabs betraying a Norse origin: those from Kilbarr, on Barra, Doid Mhairi, Port Ellen, on Islay and Inchmarnock, off Bute, are now in the Royal Museum of Scotland, Queen Street, Edinburgh. Nevertheless, despite the small number of visible Norse remains, the Hebrides were ceded to the Scottish crown as late as 1266 with the Treaty of Perth.

Argyll and the Western Isles have a rich and varied linguistic heritage in the placenames that survive from Dark Age times to the present day. It is possible to distinguish early strata among the Gaelic names which reflect the original Scottic settlement, while the Scandinavian elements testify to the strength and extent of Norse colonisation. The earliest Gaelic placenames are considered to be those containing the generic term *sliabh* meaning a hill, which is very common in Ireland and which in Scotland is concentrated in the heartlands of Dalriada, especially on Islay and Jura: *Sliabh Mor* on Islay is a very clear example. There is also a dense concentration of *sliabh* names in the Rhins of Galloway, suggesting another Scottic colony contemporary with Dalriada but apparently of no political significance. The growing influence of Gaelic-speakers in the rest of Scotland is reflected by the wide distribution of names beginning with *Kil-*, derived from Gaelic *cill* meaning cell or church; in the west, names such as Kilbarr on Barra and Kilchalman on North Uist are witness to Dalriadic expansion northwards in the seventh and eighth centuries AD.

Norse colonisation from around AD 800 is very clearly demonstrated by placenames containing the Scandinavian elements *stathr* meaning dwelling-place or farm, *setr* meaning dwelling and *bólstathr*, farm; the first two elements are frequent in the placenames of Skye and the Western Isles and are thought to represent the earliest stages of Norse settlement, while *bólstathr* names show the full extent of settlement in Western Scotland, with concentrations on Coll and Tiree, Mull and Islay. Names such as Tolsta on Lewis and Olistadh on Islay derive from *stathr*, those such as Earshader on North Uist derive from *setr*, while *bólstathr* gave rise to names such as Carbost on Skye or Cornabus on Islay.

The early medieval period saw the rise of several important families, including those we know today as the clans Donald and Dougall; in the middle of the 12th century, Somerled defeated the Norse rulers of Argyll and the Isles, and his MacDonald successors took the title of Lords of the Isles. The patronage of the leading families was an important contribution to religious foundations on Iona, and at Saddell and Ardchattan, but their most dramatic legacy has been the series of castles that are a major part of any architectural pilgrimage in the west. Royal involvement is perhaps slighter here than in any other part of Scotland, for there are no royal palaces or ecclesiastical foundations. The rise of clan Campbell stems from their support for Robert Bruce who, after defeating the MacDougalls at the Pass of Brander in 1308, transferred the forfeited MacDougall lands to Neil Campbell. Bruce visited and enlarged Tarbert Castle (no. 34) about 1326 and started the expansion of royal control in the west; in 1493 the Lordship of the Isles was finally forfeited to the crown.

The Highland chieftains played a peripheral role in politics in the centuries before 1700, although in some cases personal feuds reflected the national issues of the day. The Reformation seems to have had little architectural effect until the 18th century. Many Highland chiefs remained loyal to the Stuart family, however, even after James VII and II had fled to the continent. Remoteness from the centre of power in London, with long lines of communication, as well as the tangled politics of the Highlands, played their parts in events that culminated in the Massacre of Glencoe in 1692, infamous because of the disregard of traditional hospitality. This empty glen evokes for many what was to be the fate of much of the Highlands. Loyalty to the Jacobite cause roused many Highland clans to follow the Old Pretender in 1715 and Prince Charles Edward Stuart in 1745. The high hopes of the clans at Glenfinnan were to be dashed at Culloden in 1746. Several later memorials to the '45 are now historic monuments in their own right, including the fine memorial at Glenfinnan (NM 906805), with an adjacent National Trust for Scotland visitor-centre. A poignant early 19th century slab is that on Eilean Munde in Loch Leven (NN 083591), which shows Duncan McKenzie of North Ballachulish dismounting and killing a dragoon at the battle of Prestonpans in 1745.

In the aftermath of the '45 Government reaction was to suppress the Gaelic language, to ban the distinctive dress of the Highlander as well as the pipes, and even to abolish the old relationship between the chieftain and the clan; for the sake of peace the Highlands should be less isolated and thus brought into the economic framework of Britain as a whole. Primarily military reasons lay behind the first attempts that were made to improve communications to the west with new roads and bridges, including those built under the direction of General George Wade between 1724 and 1740 and, in our area, largely under his successor Major William Caulfield. Efforts made to improve economic conditions in the Highlands included the creation of planned towns to take advantage of the potential of fishing, for example Tobermory on Mull.

The forests of the west Highlands were exploited by iron masters from Cumbria from the 1750s, with the setting up of a furnace at Bonawe in 1753 (no. 8).

In the 18th and 19th century we can gain an impression not only of the way of life of the uppermost stratum of society at Inveraray and later Torosay, but also something of the hardship suffered by the rural population. By seeking a greater return from their estates by what were thought to be more efficient methods, but with scant regard for their tenants, many landowners sought to clear their land of the people who farmed it in traditional holdings. Overpopulation and failed harvests were also spurs to emigration to the colonies and to America or to take the King's shilling and join a Highland regiment. The Outer Isles were the scene of some of the most harrowing clearances and of resistance to them. The century between about 1750 and 1850 thus saw radical changes in the patterns of population in the Highlands that have left their mark on the architectural record today. Townships such as Auchindrain were no longer the main unit of settlement; the farm became the focus for rural activity, with small towns offering a market and a wide variety of ancillary services. The passing of the Crofters Holdings Act of 1886 gave crofters a series of basic rights, abolished the landowner's right to evict, and established for the first time security of tenure, with the promise of fair rents and an incentive to undertake improvements. At Arnol and Auchindrain and in smaller museums on Skye and South Uist, the visitor can gain some impression of the farming and building skills of country life; contemporary songs, stories and music evoke something of the pleasures, satisfactions and seasonally ordered ways of rural Scotland.

The range of the archaeological and architectural heritage of Argyll, Lochaber and the Isles has great chronological depth from earliest prehistoric times, through the medieval period with the unexpected richness of its ecclesiastical and military buildings, almost to the present day.

NINETEENTH AND EARLY TWENTIETH CENTURY ARCHITECTURE

The second half of the 19th century saw the growth of such towns as Dunoon, Oban and Stornoway with municipal buildings, some imposing hotels and churches; many other important architectural achievements of this period in the west of Scotland were the result of the building or refurbishment of many of the great country houses. Few are open to the public, though Torosay is a fine exception (no. 3). Some are already demolished or derelict, for the smooth running of such establishments demanded a host of servants, largely out of keeping with the economic demands of today. Armadale Castle, on Skye, still remains as the Clan Donald Centre (no. 1); the castle as originally conceived by James Gillespie Graham (1815-1820) with additions by David Bryce (1856-8) has been partly demolished, but the visitor can still obtain some impression of its original size and architectural embellishments. Some houses have become hotels, and the visitor to Stonefield Castle Hotel (NR 864717) can appreciate the elegant country house designed by William Playfair between 1836-8. Others remain as private homes like the fairy-tale Scots Baronial country house created by Charles Kinnear and J Dick Peddie at Glengorm Castle, Mull (NM 439572) in 1860, which forms an imposing landmark at the northern entrance to the Sound of Mull. The exteriors of several country houses can be seen with the double pleasure of visiting their gardens as part of Scotland's Garden Scheme, many Argyll gardens being at their best in May and June. Torosay and Stonefield also fall into this category; others of

architectural interest include Achnacloich (NM 955340), in rambling Scots Baronial style dating to 1885, and Benmore House, in the Younger Botanic Garden (NS 138854), another elaborate Scots Baronial mansion dating to 1862-4.

Another house, the gardens of which are open, is Ardtornish House in Morvern (NM 703475); it offers a glimpse into the working of a Highland estate in the middle and later 19th century. In Morvern many of the farms that belonged to the Duke of Argyll were sold in the years following 1819, and the succeeding proprietors have been particularly well documented. Several cleared the land to make way for sheep—a process that was already under way; indeed one of the new proprietors was Patrick Sellar, the former factor to the Sutherland estates, whose success in 'putting the mountains under Cheviot sheep' caused such notoriety. By the middle of the 19th century, Ardtornish House was not only a sheep farm but also a focus for Highland holidays for the Sellar family, before it was sold in 1860. The new laird, Octavius Smith, who already owned estates in Morvern, was by trade a distiller in London, and he may be taken as an example of the new class of proprietor of Highland estates; both Smith and his son Valentine had interests in the sporting potential of the estate, and little by little the sheep were cleared to make way for a deer 'forest'. The organisation of such a property required a factor, shepherds, game-keepers and gardeners to say nothing of the indoor staff, and they and their families required

Glengorm Castle, Mull.

17

Ardkinglas House, Cowal.

estate houses, particularly grand in the factor's case, kennels, and indeed a school for the children. Many of these buildings still remain today as testimony to the infrastructure of one aspect of life in the Highlands at this time. The present house, built between 1884-91 to designs by Alexander Ross in 'Picturesque style' and described as an outstanding example of Romanticism in architecture, is situated at the head of a small sheltered bay and is surrounded by extensive plantations of rhododendrons; as at Breachacha on Coll, the siting of the modern house at the head of Loch Aline reflects its accessibility by sea (Valentine Smith even had a steam-yacht), a factor that was as important in the 19th century as it was to the builders of the nearby medieval castles of Ardtornish and Kinlochaline (NM 691426 and NM 697476).

In contrast to the Scots Baronial style, Mountstuart on Bute (NS 108595), commissioned by the 3rd Marquess of Bute, is a magnificent evocation of several strands of European architectural traditions. Much of the central part of the 18th century mansion was destroyed by fire in 1877, and Lord Bute, whose deep interest in restoration (eg nos 32 and 51) and in building had already brought him into contact with many of the eminent architects and designers of the day, thus had the opportunity to build a new Scottish seat; the architect was R Rowand Anderson, and between 1879 and the First World War the construction and complex interior decoration were undertaken, often by craftsmen who had worked with William Burges on Bute's earlier medieval fancies at Cardiff Castle and Castell Coch in South Wales. Parallels for the intricate

Gothic decoration may be found from Segovia to Blois. For the railings of the gallery of the great hall Bute dispatched his architect to the tomb of Charlemagne at Aachen in order to make 'measured drawings . . . on the spot'. One of the most visited churches in Argyll and again a monument to High Victorian eclectic taste, although on a smaller scale, is St Conan's, Lochawe (no. 2).

Another grand vision is that of Kinloch Castle on the island of Rum (NM 401995), the residence of Sir George Bullough, a Lancashire textile-machinery magnate. The design was put to competition in the Victorian manner, and the winners were the firm of Leeming and Leeming; in 1897 the castle was built of rose-coloured stone brought from Arran to a practical design round a central courtyard, with an external glass-covered arcade to provide a sheltered walk in wet weather. Two major commissions for Robert Lorimer illustrate different approaches to the creation of a Highland mansion. In 1906 Lorimer designed a mansion in Baronial style at Ardkinglas for Sir Andrew Noble; the north-west range of the house, which held the main public rooms, offers extensive views down Loch Fyne (NN 175103). At Dunderave (1911) Lorimer's task, also for the Noble family, was to remodel a tower-house of 1596 to 20th century standards (NN 143096); wings were added to the east and south to form an entrance courtyard, but in the main the tower has retained its late medieval appearance, and, although it is not open to the public, it may be glimpsed from the road.

Mountstuart, Bute: photograph taken by Bedford Lemere.

Mountstuart, Bute: great hall, photograph taken by Bedford Lemere.

Armadale Castle, Skye:
photographed in 1965 before
partial demolition (no. 1).

1* Armadale Castle, Skye

1815-20 and 1856-8
NG 640046. Signposted, on the A 851 near the
southern tip of Skye.
Clan Donald Lands Trust.

The MacDonalds of Sleat had a house at Armadale for
some time before building a new one here as their
principal residence in 1815 when they moved from
Monkstadt (see no. 26). The 18th century mansion
house was used first as a dower house and then was
inhabited by the factor of the estate; it was here that
Flora MacDonald married Allan MacDonald, son of
the factor, in 1750. In 1815 an impressive building
designed by James Gillespie Graham was begun at the
southern end of the original mansion house, and,
although a defensive structure was no longer required,
the house was known as Armadale Castle. Forty years
later much of the original house was burnt down and
replaced by a building designed by David Bryce. In
1925 the MacDonalds moved again, to a more modest
residence at Ostaig, a little to the north, and eventually
Armadale Castle was purchased by the Clan Donald
Lands Trust. The remaining part of the old mansion
house was renovated and opened to the public as the
Clan Donald Centre. The Gillespie Graham building
became unsafe and was dismantled in 1980, leaving
only the doorway and the lower part of the main stair.
The Bryce addition remains, empty and roofless. The
photograph shows the Castle before demolition took
place.

The stable range is in a fine gothic style of 1822 and
has been converted to a restaurant and gift shop. Part
of the Castle houses an exhibition and audio-visual
display about Clan Donald, in particular during the
period of the Lordship of the Isles.
The gardens at Armadale were famous in the 18th
century, when supplies of fruit were sent to

Monkstadt. Dr Johnson, who visited Armadale in 1773,
was struck by the walled garden shaded by tall ash
trees, the plantation of which 'proves that the present
nakedness of the Hebrides is not wholly the fault of
Nature'. Further gardens were created in the 19th
century; the woodland gardens have been restored and
offer many beautiful views across the Sound of Sleat.

2* St Conan's Church, Lochawe, Lorn

1907-30
NN 115267. In Lochawe village on the A 85
between Dalmally and Taynuilt.

St Conan's Church, Lochawe, is a monument to the
skills and determination of Walter Douglas Campbell,
who had built a mansion on the island of Innis
Chonain in Loch Awe. Campbell designed and built
the first church on the site between 1881 and 1886,
occupying what is now the nave, but he envisaged a
more imposing structure; he devoted himself to the
design and building of the church between 1907 and
his death in 1914. The completion of the task was
supervised by his sister Helen and, although she died
in 1927, the church was at last dedicated in 1930.

The church is spacious and light; although designed to
juxtapose many different styles both in the interior
and in the decoration of the exterior, it is a memorable
place to visit. Fragments from Iona Abbey are
incorporated into the north wall of the south aisle, and
a window from St Mary's Parish Church, South Leith,
is built into the south wall of the Bruce Chapel. An
unusual object is also preserved in the Bruce Chapel: a
bell founded in 1843 for Skerryvore Lighthouse (no.
13).

St Conan's Church, Lochawe, Lorn;
view of chancel (no. 2).

3* Torosay Castle, Mull

1856-1900
NM 728352. Some 2 km ESE of Craignure;
narrow-gauge railway between Torosay and
Craignure.

The present Torosay Castle was completed in 1858 for
Colonel Campbell of Possil to the design of the
distinguished architect David Bryce, in Scots Baronial
style. The castle provides a vivid impression of
Victorian and Edwardian country life in the West
Highlands. The irregular crow-stepped gables and
turreted façade combine to suggest venerable antiquity. The interiors illustrate the styles
and fashions of the period, and there are several fine
portraits of the Guthrie family. The gardens are
equally remarkable, having been laid out by Robert
Lorimer in 1899; the uppermost terrace, the Fountain
Terrace, is just below the house, with The Lion Terrace
just below that. The beautiful Statue Walk is
immediately to the WSW. The statues themselves
form the largest group of 18th century Venetian pieces
to be found in Britain and were purchased in Milan
around 1900 for inclusion in the garden. They are
from the workshop of Antonio Bonazza (1698-1763)
and comprise huntsmen, gardeners, fishermen and
female figures.

Torosay Castle, Mull: from south-east (no. 3).

2

RURAL BUILDINGS

The traditional rural buildings of Argyll and Mull in the 18th and 19th century were of drystone construction with turf or thatched roofs on timber frameworks; in some cases the fittings within the house were of wickerwork or a mixture of clay and wicker.

The late 18th and early 19th century was a time of change in the way that the lairds divided up the land between their tenants, as a result of the introduction of Lowland farming methods and agricultural improvements generally. In some places larger and more efficient units were created on Lowland lines by the amalgamation of smaller holdings; in other areas crofting townships were formed to settle some of the formerly scattered agricultural families, who were cleared to make way for sheep farming, and to provide them with at least some income from the land. Some of the original holdings remained in operation, however, run along traditional lines; at Auchindrain for example the buildings of such a township are being restored to create an exciting and informative museum (no. 5).

Each summer, to allow the crops to grow unhindered, the cattle and sheep were taken to summer pasture some distance from, and usually upland of, the parent township; the summer grazing, or shieling, was often associated with a group of huts. The foundations suggest that their siting was often constant, but their roofs were probably rebuilt each season. Many shieling-huts can be found in the hills, often beside the

Kentangaval, Barra: photographed in the 1890s by Erskine Beveridge.

fork of a stream; the illustrated shieling-hut foundations are from a group at Malcolm's Bridge on Rum (NM 354983).

On Tiree and in the Western Isles the houses are of a distinctive form known as the blackhouse, perhaps best seen at Arnol on the west side of Lewis (no. 4); a hollow-wall construction was preferred, with an inner and an outer stone face and earth filling the space between. The air photograph of the township illustrates the strip pattern of fields and plots of each croft. This was also a feature of land-holding on St Kilda, and, in view of the exceptional nature of what is one of the most remote of the properties of the National Trust for Scotland, a special section has been included on the island (no. 7). A croft has been described as 'a piece of land entirely surrounded by regulations'. It is indeed a piece of land, of less than 75 acres (about 30 hectares), with an annual rent of less than £50. The tenant has the right to leave the tenancy to an heir, or to assign it to a stranger, subject to the approval of the Crofters Commission. The landlord has a limited right to resume occupancy of the land. Any house, outbuildings and other improvements are erected and maintained by the crofter (the tenant), but, since he does not own the land, should the croft revert to the landlord or the tenancy be sold, compensation is paid for the buildings which stand on it. Generally crofts are grouped in townships, and each township has available in common a larger area of land, parts of which may be suitable for cultivation, the rest being

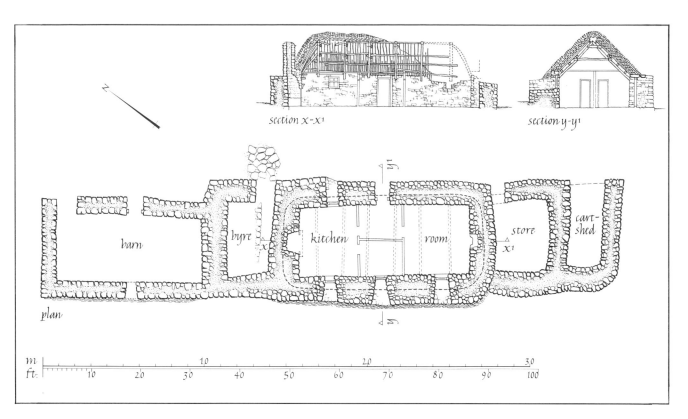

section x-x¹ section y-y¹

barn byre kitchen room store cart-shed

plan

m | 1,0 2,0 3,0
ft: | 10 20 30 40 50 60 70 80 90 100

Ruaig, Tiree: plan and sections of croft-house and steading.

used for grazing. The number and type of stock which a crofter may have on the common grazing varies from one township to another according to the area and quality of the pasture and the pressure on the grazing. In a few places arable land is still held on the run-rig system, by which a person will have a different area or a different group of strips each year, but in most townships the arable ground is now permanently apportioned to individual crofts and the areas are fenced. There is an increasing tendency on the part of crofters to apply for a permanent allocation of a portion of the common grazing land which is then fenced and improved by regular applications of sand, basic slag, fertiliser and seed. On suitable ground this can increase the carrying capacity by tenfold. The

contrast between the emerald green of good improved grazing and the darker colours of the moorland vegetation on the other side of the fence is often very striking. Some individuals may hold several crofts, but rarely is the croft or group of crofts the sole source of income; most households have at least one other source: fishing, teaching, nursing, fish-farming or weaving, employment in the construction industry, often on a casual basis, or, as in many cases, an old age pension. A number of grants and subsidies are available to encourage full and efficient use of the land: annual sums are paid per breeding ewe and per head of hill cattle, though these do not always cover the cost of extra winter feeding; grants are given for fencing, for improving pasture and for the cultivation of some crops. The high cost of transport to and from the mainland can be an inhibiting factor, depressing the sale price of stock which have to be taken to the mainland for re-sale for slaughter or fattening, and increasing the price of imported commodities such as artificial fertiliser and hay. The crofter now has the right to buy his croft for a comparatively small sum, with some restrictions on subsequent resale, but few have done this, for the disadvantages outweigh the advantages in many cases.

Tangy Mill, Kintyre.

Many of the buildings associated with 'improved' agriculture are also impressive or interesting in their own right, but as these are often still in use as farmhouses, barns and byres we have not included any as monuments to be visited. In some areas estate owners built farms and steadings to standard patterns that remain visible to this day—the octagonal horse-gangs of Colonsay are still a striking feature of the island. The unusual D-shaped plan of the farmsteading at Kilchiaran, Islay (NR 206603), which dates to about

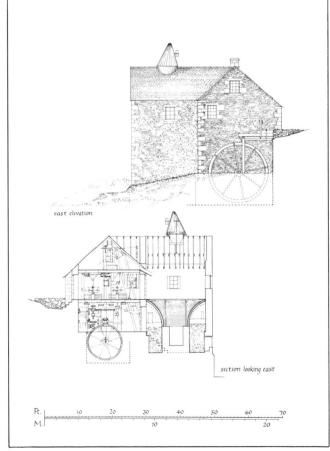

east elevation

section looking east

| Ft. | 10 | 20 | 30 | 40 | 50 | 60 | 70 |
| M. | | 10 | | | 20 | | |

Ardheisker, North Uist.

Eilean a' Ghiorr, North Uist: photographed in the 1890s by Erskine Beveridge.

*Malcolm's Bridge, Rum:
shielings.*

1826, can be appreciated from the road; the steading contains the barn and mill on its N side, with the water-wheel powered from a mill-pond immediately to the N. The early 19th century mill at Tangy, Kintyre, may be visited by prior appointment (NR 662277); this three-storey mill houses the complex machinery of grinding and threshing as well as drying the grain, and it was in operation until 1961. In rather the same way that the Highland estate was the focus of one aspect of the rural economy, we may envisage the mill and the livestock market as the centres of a prosperous agricultural economy for other parts of the area, notably Kintyre. A headstone illustrating a plough-team in Killean churchyard (no. 46) is an example of a local group of sculpture that evokes this aspect of farming life. Arnol and Auchindrain (nos 4 and 5) illustrate two entirely different, but contemporary, strands in this complex pattern of landholding in Argyll and the Western Isles.

4* Arnol Blackhouse, Lewis

c 1870

NB 310492. Signposted on the A 858: there are two roads which join in Arnol township and lead to the blackhouse which is about 1 km from the main road.

HBM (SDD).

Few blackhouses in the islands are still inhabited, and not many are maintained: straw thatch needs regular attention and renewal, although heather thatch can last for decades. When a house is not properly heated and the roof is allowed to fall in, it can deteriorate rapidly, but fortunately at least one of these old houses, with its outbuildings, is now preserved. The visitor can see clearly how buildings and areas with a variety of functions (dwelling, byre, barn and peat store) are all under adjoining roofs, a sensible arrangement in an adverse climate. The small number of windows and doors keeps draughts to a minimum; the thick double walls with earth and midden between them keep out not only the weather but even the sound of the storms. This house was built in the late 19th century and does not have some of the features seen in earlier houses, such as the rounded outer corners, which were designed to reduce wind resistance. Rain runs down the roof and into the thickness of the walls, keeping the soil between the inner and outer skins damp and thus both helping to hold it together and keeping the wind out; the stones of the inner face are laid with a slope on the upper surface, to discourage the damp from entering the house. The roof is thatched, straw over sods on a timber frame, the rafters placed on the inner face of the wall. At one time the soot impregnated straw was removed annually and used for dressing the arable land. The flat area around the edge of the roof, on top of the wall, facilitates thatching and repairs; steps built into the outside wall allow easy access.

Cattle and people shared the same entrance, separating inside—cattle to a byre on the right, with wooden stalls and a box-pen for calves. A central drain runs out through the end wall. People turned to the left, into a living room, with a fire in the centre of the flagged floor, a settle on one side, on the other a dresser and cupboards. Stools provided extra seating. Cooking was done on a girdle beside the hearth or in pots hanging from a chain fastened to the rafters; hooks allowed the pots to hang at varying distances from the fire for boiling or simmering. There is no chimney or hole for the smoke. Beyond the living area are the box beds; the thatch was rarely totally efficient, and box beds kept out any draughts or rain that might penetrate. Before restoration most of the walls and parts of the ceiling in these two areas were papered. A door opposite the main entrance gives access to the adjoining building which was used as a barn. In the back wall is a low aperture, blocked now, in line with the passage between house and byre; this provided a draught for winnowing on the floor of the barn. This central area was used for a variety of purposes—storing fleeces or potatoes, and keeping foodstuffs for stock. Some agricultural tools were also kept here. To the left is a wooden floored area where the sheaves were piled, tossed through a hole opened in the roof. At the other end is a partitioned area, used as a store for dry peats, and as a shelter at lambing time.

Outside the house is a walled stackyard.

Water was taken from springs, which generally have a built stone cover. These springs or wells could be some distance from the houses which relied on them. Lighting was provided, before the advent of electricity, by paraffin lamps.

There are a number of houses in Arnol which show the main structural features seen in the museum, and in many other townships blackhouses or remains of blackhouses may be seen: there are, for instance, two at Callanish (NB 213335 and NB 213331); the plan of a roofless example can be seen fairly well from Dun Carloway Broch (no. 61) and at Garenin (NB 192442)

Arnol Blackhouse, Lewis (no. 4).

Arnol Blackhouse, Lewis: showing rear barn and walled stackyard (no. 4).

AUCHINDRAIN

*Auchindrain, Mid Argyll: plan of
northern part of township (no. 5)*

there is an unusual group, now very dilapidated. Here several houses have been built close together on either side of a track; some have undergone later alterations, including the construction of stone gables.

5* Auchindrain Township, Mid Argyll
19th century.
NN 0303. Signposted on south side of A 83 (Inveraray to Lochgilphead road) 8 km south-west of Inveraray. Trustees of Auchindrain Museum.

Even in 1845 it was recorded that the quantity of rain which falls in this parish of Inveraray is 'prodigious', and it is important to choose a good day to visit the restored township of Auchindrain in order to make the most of the scattered buildings, many furnished in meticulous detail. As it stands today Auchindrain illustrates the type of joint-tenancy holding that would have been common around 1800 and indeed before. Twelve tenants paid their rent jointly to the Duke of Argyll and each had a share of the arable land, by dividing it into strips or rigs, and also of the common grazing. The number of rigs to be worked and the number of beasts each tenant was allowed to graze was determined by his share in the tenancy. Auchindrain thus shows the way the land was worked before the adoption of large-scale sheep-farming from the later part of the 18th century onward. The families remained the Duke's tenants, and the fields and slopes were not enclosed by the massive dykes of the lowland farmers. Thus Auchindrain remained until about 1935, and the last tenant lived in house A until 1954.

There are twenty buildings in the complex: houses, longhouses (byre and dwelling combined), barns, sheds and stables, and an excellent display in the information centre sets the scene before one ventures out to the township buildings. Most have drystone walls with the roof supported on cruck-frames and employing turf, straw or heather thatch, though several were replaced with corrugated iron in the early 20th century. Building N, immediately to the north-east of the modern house, is a barn with adjacent stackyard; the opposing doorways are to provide a through draught for winnowing. The adjacent little house (M), probably built in the 1870s, is the equivalent of today's sheltered housing, for if the

Auchindrain, Mid Argyll: House H, parlour interior (no. 5)

Auchindrain, Mid Argyll: interior of byre of House A (no. 5).

village supported an indigent person it was exempted from paying the Poor Rate. K is a shed currently with a display of smith's tools. J, H and D are longhouses with D perhaps the oldest in the township. House H has been furnished to show what it would have been like in the 1890s. House A on the other hand is probably the most recent, dating to about 1820; the arrangement of living and byre accommodation gives a good impression of what a country cottage of the middle of the last century looked like. The ingenious method of restraining cattle in the byre is shown in the photograph: one of a pair of upright posts could be moved to allow the cow's head into the gap, and the post was then pegged back into position. Several of the buildings on the south-east side of the little burn that runs through the township are currently being restored, and visitors can see the various building-and roofing-techniques of the past being put into practice.

There are several isolated kailyards or walled kitchen gardens, which produced both green vegetables for the community and also fruit; sometimes flax was grown.

One important aspect of the west Highland economy cannot be shown at Auchindrain—the summer shieling; the cattle were taken away from the township so that they should not trample on the growing crops, and between June and August many of the women and old folk would have tended the cattle in the hills on either side of the Douglas Water where the township had its summer grazings, and where the shieling-huts were made ready each year by an advance party.

Keils, Jura: aerial view (no. 6).

6　Keils, Jura
19th century.
NR 524683. Signposted on the west side of the A 846 just north of Craighouse.

The little crofting township of Keils on Jura may be taken as a typical example of the smaller settlement unit in many parts of the west Highlands. The air photograph shows the layout of the houses, byres and barns. The stackyard illustrates the type of stone foundation for small haystacks that was once common in Argyll; the interior of the byre, now sadly dilapidated, shows the method of construction of the cruck-framed roof—the crucks springing from the wall with the supporting cross-timbers near the ridge. The drain, however, is not original, and there is little doubt that this byre was built as a longhouse comparable to those at Auchindrain, partly as a dwelling and partly as a stalled byre.

Keils, Jura: stackyard (no. 6).

Keils, Jura: interior of byre (no. 6).

35

St Kilda: view of the street with cleits behind (no. 7).

7 St Kilda

19th century.

NF 1099. 55 km west-north-west of the Sound of Harris. Contact the National Trust for Scotland for information about staying on the island. All visitors should report to the Nature Conservancy Council warden on landing.

The St Kilda archipelago consists of the four islands of Hirta, Dun, Soay and Boreray, with associated stacks and islets; it belongs to the National Trust for Scotland and is leased to the Nature Conservancy Council as a National Nature Reserve. A small portion of Hirta is sub-let to the Ministry of Defence.

The date of the earliest settlement of the islands is not known, but it is clear from documentary evidence that there was a community living there by medieval times. There are very few structures which can definitely be attributed to any period earlier than the 19th century, and it is the village complex laid out in the 1830s which immediately impresses the visitor upon entering Village Bay. The resident minister at that time, offended by the squalid habitations of his parishioners, persuaded them to build new homes. The arable land, which had until then been divided into numerous strips that were re-allocated every three years, was permanently apportioned in a pattern of strips radiating from the curve of the shore; the new houses were built along a street curving behind the shore and the whole was surrounded by a head-dyke. The small houses were of the blackhouse type, with the family living at one end and the cattle in the byre at the other end. In the 1860s these houses were given over entirely to cattle and storage, the families moving into new mortared buildings, which were more spacious, although in some ways less practical, for they faced the bay and therefore the worst of the weather; they also had thin walls and zinc roofs, which caused severe condensation, but after the roofs blew off tarred felt was found to be more satisfactory.

Near the rocks which were used as a landing place is a two-storey building used to store the commodities accumulated to pay the rent: tweed, oil, fish, and feathers. A little further along the shore is the manse and church, built in 1828 to plans by Robert Stevenson; a schoolroom was built onto the church in 1900. Another two-storey building was the house where the factor stayed during his annual visit to collect the rent, and in the late 19th century this house was also used by teachers and various visitors, and in this century by the district nurse. Just behind the village street is an oval walled graveyard. There is now no trace of Christ's Church, which stood here in medieval times, although a stone with a cross cut into it, presumably of medieval date, is built into the front wall of Cottage 16 at the west end of the street, and another cross forms part of the ceiling of a cleit behind the village.

Not far from the burial ground is a short underground passage or souterrain, similar to some found in the Western Isles and on the mainland. Sherds of iron-age pottery have been found in this structure.

Behind the village and outside the head-dyke are several beehive-shaped structures. There is evidence that smaller cells were built adjacent to these, with a connecting passage. These buildings may include elements of the houses in use before 1830.

Scattered within the village and over large areas of the surrounding hills are many drystone buildings called cleits. These have parallel walls enclosing a narrow space, rounded ends, and a door at the end facing uphill or occasionally on one side. The roof lintels are covered with stones capped with earth and turf. The thick roof prevents the rain penetrating, but the air circulated between the walls, drying anything inside. These buildings were used for storage; in the village area they contained a variety of things—birds, fish, hay and turf; on the hills many still contain pieces of turf cut for fuel. Throughout their recorded history, the

St Kilda: view of the village and cleits (no. 7).

islanders depended to a great extent for their food on the sea birds which thronged the cliffs and slopes; the large populations of puffins, gannets and fulmars were harvested on a scale unknown elsewhere in Britain.

On the north side of the island in Gleann Mor another type of building is found—a small walled court with two or three small adjoining cells; low walls form a funnel-like entrance to the court. There are about twenty of these structures in the floor of the Glen. Latterly they were used as shielings, although it is possible that they were originally built for another purpose. Also in Gleann Mor is the Amazon's House, a complex beehive construction, now very dilapidated. It is referred to by Martin Martin, who visited the islands in 1697, as the House of the Female Warrior—reputed to have been a princess from Harris.

There are more cleits and bothies on Boreray, Soay and Stac an Armin, but it is difficult to land on these islands, and, while there was seasonal occupation on Boreray, it is very doubtful if they were ever permanently inhabited.

The maximum recorded population was 180 at the end of the 17th century, when the islands supported a thriving community. Disease and emigration reduced the numbers until in the early 20th century there was no longer a viable population, and the islanders asked for Government assistance to be resettled. They were evacuated from the island in August 1930. Twenty seven years later the islands were given to the National Trust for Scotland, and the Ministry of Defence established a base on Hirta to track missiles fired from the rocket testing-station in South Uist and to ensure safety in the range area during firing.

St Kilda: a cleit (no. 7).

St Kilda: cross on Cottage 16 (no. 7)

40

3

INDUSTRIAL MONUMENTS

In recent times, one of the greatest natural assets of mainland Argyll has been its forests, vast reserves of timber which, in the 18th century, attracted the rapidly expanding iron industry as an easily available source of fuel. Iron furnaces survive from this period at Bonawe and Furnace, that at Bonawe (no. 8) being specially worth a visit as a most dramatic and well-preserved industrial monument, which illustrates the whole process of using charcoal to smelt iron-ore.

Seaweed was probably gathered and used as a fertiliser long before its commercial value was realised. In 1735 the kelp industry was started by Clanranald in North Uist; seaweed was collected, dried and burned to produce an ash which was used in the manufacture of glass, soap and linen. This was taken up in Harris, Lewis, Skye and Mull. The price rose during the latter part of the 18th century when supplies of soda ash from the continent were cut off, and though it fell again towards the end of the 18th century, it was not until the 1820s that cheaper sources of soda put an end to the kelp industry, creating much misery in the islands. As prices had risen, the lairds had encouraged the growth of the industry, and though they and the middlemen took a great proportion of the wealth, some was returned to those who did the work. The loss of income when the kelp industry failed suddenly meant great hardship for many and was one of the causes of the major emigrations of the 19th century. Traces of this industry can still be seen in some places;

small hollows by the shore may be overgrown kelp-kilns, in which the seaware was burned.

On land, the rocks have been quarried profitably in some places, slate being one of the best examples; the slate islands—Seil, Luing, Shuna and Easdale, together with Ballachulish, once supplied most of the slate for western Scotland and exported to England and America. Granite was quarried at Fionnphort and freestone at Carsaig, both in Mull, feldspar in Harris and ironstone in Raasay. Machrihanish, in Kintyre, was the centre of thriving coal working from the late 18th century until 1967. Perhaps the most enduring architectural contribution of the slate quarries are the villages of quarriers' dwellings for example at Easdale and Ellanbeich; most date to the early 19th century and comprise two main rooms, probably both originally containing beds. The compact layout of two back-to-back rows of houses of the main part of the village can be seen in the photograph, as well as the flooded quarry workings.

At one time the distilling of whisky was a normal domestic occupation, particularly after the introduction of potatoes which partially supplanted barley in the diet, and released a proportion of the barley crop to be used in the still. When the duty was lowered in 1822, illicit distilling was no longer worthwhile; there are now a small number of commercial distilleries.

Clachan Bridge, Seil, Lorn.

Dunoon Pier, Conal.

Several important monuments of industrial archaeology have had a part in improving communications between the west of Scotland and the south. The modern motorist, hardly changing gear up the Rest and be Thankful, coasting through Glen Lochy, or crossing the causeways linking several of the Western Isles, enjoys the last stage of the opening up of the Scottish Highlands. The first was the creation of military roads and bridges beginning in 1725: by the 1780s there were about a thousand such roads in the Highlands. Bridges and piers were improved, in the case of Clachan Bridge (NM 785197), completed in 1791, linking the island of Seil with the mainland of Argyll, hence its nickname—'Bridge over the Atlantic'. Piers such as that at Lagg, Jura (NR 598785) illustrate

the skills of the builders in the use of drystone techniques, with the upper surface of vertically set blocks above horizontally set outer and inner walls. The next stage was the building of the Crinan and the Caledonian Canals following Acts of Parliament in 1793 and 1803 respectively; the canals are described in greater detail later (nos 9 and 10). The expansion of steamer services, particularly in the second half of the 19th century, necessitated the building of many elaborate piers, such as that at Dunoon, rebuilt in 1896, but also initiated a tourist industry that required the hotels and boarding-houses that are a feature of sea-fronts from Rothesay to Oban. The terrain was hardly favourable to the supporters of the growth of the railway network into the west, but with feats of

Easdale and Ellanbeich, Lorn: slate quarries and workers' dwellings.

engineering ingenuity railways were brought to Oban, and for a while to Ballachulish. The former rail bridge at Connel (NM 910345) still survives in a converted form as a key link for road traffic; Connel Bridge, built between 1901 and 1903, has the second largest cantilever span in the country (152.5 m). Fort William, Mallaig, Fort Augustus and Kyle of Lochalsh joined the Railway Age, and several magnificent viaducts are still in use at Auch (NN 335362) between Tyndrum and Bridge of Orchy, and at Glenfinnan (NM 910813). The Glenfinnan viaduct, opened in 1901, has twenty-one spans for its length of 380 m, and is constructed of mass-concrete. Taynuilt Station (NN 003311), built in 1879, with the main offices on one platform and originally a small wooden shelter on the other, is a typical example of highland railway stations. There are

slight traces of the canal and later the light railway that served the coal mines near Machrihanish, first at Drumlemble and latterly at Machrihanish itself. The canal was in operation between the 1790s and the middle of the 19th century. The building of the colliery railway began in 1876, and in 1906, extended and improved, the line opened as the Campbeltown and Machrihanish Light Railway Company in order to cater for passenger and tourist traffic. Competition from buses brought the line to a close in 1937. Today's roads, with several elegant modern bridges to delight future generations of industrial archaeologists, are largely the result of the demands of fast commercial and private transport between the towns of the west and the industrial south of Scotland.

Bonawe Iron Furnace, Lorn: cast-iron lintel (no. 8).

Bonawe Iron Furnace, Lorn: furnace (no. 8).

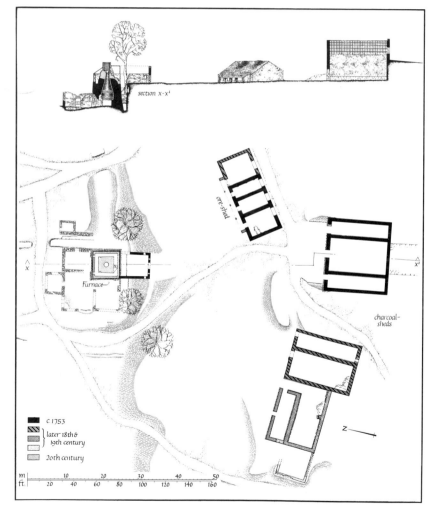

44

IRON FURNACES

8* Bonawe Iron Furnace, Lorn

Mid 18th century.
NN 009318. The furnace is well signposted from
the village of Taynuilt on the A 85 some 24 km
east of Oban.
HBM (SDD).

At a time when transport costs are perhaps one of the
most contentious issues in the Highlands it is ironic
that in the middle of the 18th century it was more
economical to ship haematite ore from Cumbria to
Loch Etive side for smelting and then to transport the
iron back to the industrial centres around the Irish
Sea, than it was to transport the enormous quantities
of charcoal necessary to the Lake District. The key was
the cheapness and availability of timber for charcoal,
and a visit to the furnace at Bonawe should be coupled
with a walk through the National Nature Reserve at
Glen Nant to the south, where the types of timber and
the platforms on which the charcoal was produced can
still be seen.

The furnace complex embodies a building style quite
unlike the architecture of the west of Scotland,
betraying the Lake District origins of the company that
established it in 1753. The centre of operations was the
furnace itself, but to appreciate the flow of operations
the tour should begin on the uppermost terrace where
the iron-ore shed and charcoal sheds are situated. The
charcoal sheds are built into the natural slope to allow
loading from a higher level behind and unloading
from a lower level at the front where there is access to
the furnace. The sheds are high and airy (to keep the
charcoal dry) with impressive timber and slate roofs.
The iron-ore shed is of two periods of construction:
the three storage bays to the south-east belong to the
earlier period, and the extension to the north-east is
rather later. Again the ore was unloaded from the
track at the rear of the shed and then barrowed from
the front doors to the furnace itself.

The furnace is situated in such a way as to allow the
constituents of the smelting process to be inserted into
the loading-mouth from one level, while the water-
wheel and lade, which powered the bellows at the base
of the furnace-stack, were on a lower terrace. The
charcoal, burning with the aid of the bellows (or
latterly a blowing-engine) at the base of the stack, was
covered with iron ore and limestone tipped in from
the top; the heat changed the iron ore into molten
iron, while the limestone flux above absorbed
impurities and could be run off as molten slag. Both
metal and slag were run off through the western of the
great openings at the base of the furnace into a casting
house where the metal was cast into pig-iron and the
slag removed to form huge heaps (in the area now
occupied by the car park). The two openings at the
base of the furnace stack are lintelled partly in
sandstone and partly by cast-iron beams, three of
which have the inscription 'BUNAW. F. [Bonawe
Furnace] 1753'; it seems likely that the lintels were cast
in the Lake District in readiness for the building of the
furnace, and the sandstone lintels were probably also
brought from Cumbria in order to ensure the smooth
construction of this crucial building.

To the north of the main complex is the L-shaped
block that formed the workers' dwellings, and to the
east is a further row of workers' dwellings and Bonawe
House, built in the later 18th century as the residence
of the company's local manager, but none of these
buildings is in the care of the Secretary of State for
Scotland, and there is no public access.

Charcoal-burning stances are a little-visited class of
monument found on many of the formerly wooded
slopes of Argyll. The platforms, measuring about 8 m
in diameter, were partly dug back into the hill-side and
partly built up on the down slope with the material
thus quarried. On this level base logs were carefully
stacked round a central stake and the pile was covered
with earth; the stake was then removed and the pile
set alight. The transformation of wood to charcoal

took up to ten days. There are good charcoal-burning stances in Glen Nant (parking at NN 019273), and spectacular though less accessible platforms are to be found at the head of Glen Etive, above the west shore of Loch Etive; these have been cut back into the slope with the down-hill side revetted by large boulders. There are about twenty platforms on this now bare hill-side, a telling reminder that the slopes were once heavily wooded (NN 1044).

Another furnace went into production at Furnace on Loch Fyne side (NN 025000) by agreement between the Duke of Argyll and a Lake District company; the furnace stack can still be viewed from the outside. One of the lintels above the bellows opening is cast, like those at Bonawe, with the name, or in this case initials, of the operating company and the date: 'GF 1755' (Goatfield Furnace).

Bonawe Iron Furnace, Lorn: ore-shed (no. 8).

CANALS

9 Caledonian Canal, Lochaber
Early 19th century.
Two sections of the Canal fall within the scope of this volume: one runs from Corpach on Loch Linnhe (NN 095766) to Gairlochy on Loch Lochy (NN 181846), with Neptune's Staircase and a railway swing-bridge centred at Banavie (NN 113770); the second runs from Laggan Locks on Loch Lochy (NN 285962) to Laggan Swing Bridge on Loch Oich (NN 300983).
British Waterways Board.

The Caledonian Canal takes advantage of the geological fault that runs from Inverness to Fort William and forms the Great Glen with three long thin lochs occupying much of the valley floor–Lochs Lochy, Oich and Ness. The line of the canal was surveyed by Thomas Telford in 1801 and 1802 and work went ahead, following an Act of Parliament in 1803, initially on the terminal basins. The impressive size of the locks seems to have been determined by the need to allow passage not only of 32-gun frigates but also of trading vessels, for part of the impetus for building the canal was the danger to west coast shipping by French pirates during the Napoleonic

Caledonian Canal, Lochaber, with Loch Lochy in the background (no. 9).

Caledonian Canal, Lochaber: sailing ships at Corpach in the 1890s photographed by Erskine Beveridge (no. 9).

Wars. The Caledonian Canal can accommodate vessels of almost twice the size of those carried by the Crinan Canal. Locks were grouped at least in part to avoid expense, but for the visitor this adds to the visual impact of the locks—eight of which form what has become known as 'Neptune's Staircase' at Banavie for example. To the south of Gairlochy, at NN 149817, the canal is carried over the River Loy by aqueduct, the facings of which are of Ballachulish granite. The canal necessitated earthworks on a massive scale such as those south of Gairlochy at NN 148816 and a huge cutting at Laggan (NN 286965); this section of canal and the adjacent shallow parts of Loch Oich were the scene of the earliest use of bucket-dredgers in a project of this type.

The many problems attendant on such an undertaking conspired to delay completion of the canal until 1822, but reconstruction and renovation continued for the rest of the century; now it is mainly used by fishing boats, yachts and a small number of trading vessels. Sailing ships, such as those shown in the illustration of canal life at Corpach, taken in the 1890s by the distinguished amateur photographer Erskine Beveridge, might be towed through the various stages of the canal by a team of tug-boats.

Arnol Village, Lewis: aerial view (no. 4).

St Kilda: Village Bay (no. 7).

Crinan Canal, Mid Argyll: aerial view of Locks 9-13 at Dunardry (no. 10).

10 Crinan Canal, Mid Argyll

Early 19th century.

The Canal runs from Ardrishaig (NR 853852) to Crinan (NR 788943) with easy access for visitors at the basins and locks at each end; there is limited parking at Cairnbaan, and, in order to view the locks of the central section, it is pleasant to walk from there along the tow path on the north side of the canal rather than to follow the main road on the south side.

British Waterways Board.

The Crinan Canal, running between Ardrishaig on Loch Fyne and Crinan near the Sound of Jura, is one of the most captivating engineering monuments in the west; the passage of yachts or the occasional puffer provides a ready opportunity to see the locks and bridges in action. The canal, authorized by an Act of Parliament in May 1793, was designed to allow passage between the Clyde and the north-west of Scotland, particularly the fisheries of the Hebrides, without rounding the treacherous Mull of Kintyre. Although the narrow neck of land might seem an ideal

Crinan Canal, Mid Argyll: Lock 2, Ardrishaig (no. 10).

Crinan Canal, Mid Argyll: Lock 2, Ardrishaig (no. 10).

location for a canal, topographical considerations combined to make the project a difficult one to complete. The unstable nature of Crinan Moss meant that the canal had to be cut into the hill-side to the south, an expensive and time-consuming procedure, which has also given the canal a tortuous route in this section. The canal had many structural problems to overcome before being opened in 1801, although only finally complete in 1809, and even then extensive repairs had to be undertaken almost immediately, Thomas Telford was in charge of renovations in 1816.

The canal is 14.5 km long and has three main sections, with the central summit between the locks at Cairnbaan and Dunardry. These locks and the locks and basins at Crinan and Ardrishaig are the main centres of canal activity. (There is ready car parking at the basins.) The rock-cut basin at Ardrishaig is now entered by a sea-lock, which was added in 1930-2, and the former lock may be seen as an inlet parallel to the new one. The canal is fed from lochs in the hills to the south, a series of reservoirs which permit water catchment from a wide area; to avoid the canal becoming over-full an ingenious automatic system of letting off the water was introduced at Ardrishaig in 1895, known as the 'water waster'. After Lock 4 the canal leads to Oakfield where there is an attractive swing bridge and the wharf which formed Lochgilphead's access to the canal. A length of the canal banks was breached in January 1805 by sudden flooding at a point about 2 km NNW of Oakfield Bridge. Although a new stretch was cut, the banks of the original canal can still be seen today (NR 851894; keep to the east tow-path). The main groups of locks on either side of the summit-reach are good view points, though parking near Dunardry is more difficult; here spanning Lock 11 is the unusual traversing bridge, an elegant, almost toy-like, cantilever structure, which may be wound backwards and forwards along rails to allow access to the north side of the canal. Crinan basin which is frequently bustling with yachts, forms a good conclusion to a tour of the canal.

LIGHTHOUSES

Until the end of the 18th century there was nothing to help those sailing the Scottish coasts at night or in misty conditions, except for the occasional beacon privately maintained. Many vessels foundered, particularly on unfamiliar coasts. In 1786 the Northern Lighthouse Trust was established, with the intention of building four lighthouses, one of which was at the Mull of Kintyre (NR 587084), and one on Eilean Glas, Scalpay, Harris (NG 247947). After overcoming extraordinary difficulties in organising the transport of skilled men and materials to these two remote places, Thomas Smith of Edinburgh installed his new purpose-built lights with reflectors; these were lit in 1788 and 1789. The light mechanism from Eilean Glas is now on display in the Royal Scottish Museum, Edinburgh. The Trust's engineer, Thomas Smith, took Robert Stevenson, his stepson, into partnership, thus beginning the long lasting connection between the Northern Lighthouse Board and the Stevenson family. Successive generations designed and built lights all round the Scottish coasts throughout the nineteenth and early twentieth centuries, incorporating many original designs and improvements of their own into their work. They were also very concerned about the welfare of the men who worked for them, both in the construction of the buildings, and subsequently in tending the lights, and apart from devoting great care to the details of the lighthouse itself, they took trouble over the provision of accommodation for the keepers and their stores, even to the securing of grazing rights for their beasts.

Ardnamurchan Lighthouse, Lochaber: view from south-east (no. 11).

The erection of the light on Skerryvore was a major achievement (no. 13). As early as 1804, Robert Stevenson had recommended that a light should be placed on this treacherous rock, but it was not until 1837 that Alan Stevenson was asked to design and build a lighthouse. Because the rock is washed by the Atlantic the work took several seasons, and the landing of man and materials could only be acccomplished in calm weather. A base was established at Hynish, on Tiree, where the keepers' dwellings were to be. Most of the stone was quarried on Mull and precisely shaped at Hynish before being shipped to the rock. A barrack was put up on stilts on the rock, providing shelter overnight and during some terrifying storms which lasted for days. All work had to be abandoned in the winter, and it was not until 1842 that the building was completed; the light was installed in the following year and was officially lit in February 1844.

Alan Stevenson also built the lights at Ardnamurchan (1849) (no. 11); Sanda (1850) and Arnish (1853), and his brothers, David and Thomas, built no less than fourteen in Argyll and the Isles, including those at Ushenish, Isle Ornsay and Rubha nan Gall (Sound of Mull) in 1857, Butt of Lewis (1862) and Dhu Heartach (1862), another perilous rock similar to the Skerryvore. Charles and D Alan Stevenson, the son and grandson of David, continued with the building tradition, and their work includes the Flannan light (1899). Many of these lights are now automatic, but those which are readily accessible are still generally manned, and it is often possible to visit them, at the discretion of the keepers.

11 Ardnamurchan Lighthouse, Lochaber
19th century.
NM 415674. At the tip of Ardnamurchan Point at the western extremity of the Ardnamurchan peninsula, signposted from Kilchoan.
Northern Lighthouse Board.

Impressive both from the sea when rounding Ardnamurchan Point or when approached by land at the most western tip of the British mainland, the lighthouse was designed by Alan Stevenson in 1846 and completed some three years later; it was one of the last of the series of great stone towers to be built by the Commissioners of the Northern Lighthouse Board. The lighthouse tower has a height of 28 m at which point the parapet walk surrounds the light-room; the tower and keepers' houses were designed on opposing sides of a courtyard with further accommodation in a rather uninspiring low block. The main architectural features of note are the Classical doorway at the base of the tower and the arched base of the upper parapet. In the light-room the original lens mechanism and mounting may still be seen.

Ardnamurchan Lighthouse, Lochaber: entrance to tower (no. 11)

12 Rinns of Islay Lighthouse, Orsay, Islay
19th century.
NR 163514. Situated on Orsay Island opposite Port Wemyss; good views from Islay.
Northern Lighthouse Board.

The Rinns of Islay Lighthouse on Orsay island at the western tip of Islay was designed by Robert Stevenson and constructed in 1824-5. The principal features of the lighthouse are the storied tower with the lightkeepers' houses and a storehouse laid out to form a courtyard. The lighting of a beacon was not always a sufficient guide to mariners, for they often had to be able to differentiate one light from another; and Stevenson created a mechanism for the Rinns of Islay light that was alternately stationary and revolving, producing what was described as a bright 'flush' of light every twelve seconds 'without those intervals of darkness which characterise other lights on the coast'.

The weights of the mechanism that created the turning of the light were formerly a feature of the central well of the spiral staircase that led to the light-room. Along with the lights at Buchan Ness and Little Ross Island, at the entrance to Kirkcudbright Bay, Lord Kelvin described the Rinns of Islay as 'undoubtedly the three best revolving lights in the world'. The other main lights on Islay are those of Ruvaal (NR 425791), completed in 1859, MacArthur's Head and Loch Indaal completed in 1861 and 1869.

Pride in the traditions of the Northern Lighthouse Board may be seen in a memorial stone in Kilchoman burial-ground (NR 216632), where there is an evocative representation of the Board's emblem with a commemoration presumably to a member of the family of the assistant keeper of the Rinns of Islay lighthouse in 1845.

Port Wemyss and Rinns of Islay. Lighthouse, Orsay, Islay (no. 12).

Rinns of Islay Lighthouse, Orsay, Islay, (no. 12)

Lightkeeper's headstone, Kilchoman Parish Church, Islay (no. 12).

reef in 1814 in the company of Robert Stevenson, he described a 'long ridge of rocks (chiefly under water), on which the tide breaks in a most tremendous style'. 'Our rowers, however, get the boat into a quiet creek between two rocks where we contrive to land well wetted.' Such were the problems of the situation that it was not until 1834 and 1835 that the survey of the reef was undertaken. The hardships of the various seasons of work on the rock with the wind whistling and the waves foaming round are a constant feature of Stevenson's account of the building. The foundation pit for such a massive tower took twenty men over two hundred days! The tower is 42 m in height rising in a gentle curve from a basal diameter of 12.8 m, and first showed its light on 1 February 1844.

If the lighthouse itself remains a distant pencil on the horizon, the shore establishment and harbour, from which workmen and stone were shipped out to the reef, can still be seen. Here each stone was carefully prepared and shaped for its special position within the structure. It had been intended to use local stone, a hard gneiss, but this proved difficult to work and, although the bottom three courses of the tower are of Hynish stone, the remainder are of Ross of Mull granite.

The well-built pier, dock, storehouses and shore-barracks for the masons and seamen still survive, as well as a signal-tower and a row of lightkeepers' houses. The signal-tower has been refurbished as a museum, with details of the building of Skerryvore and of the method of communication by semaphore signals, seen through telescopes, between the tower at Hynish and the lighthouse.

An unexpected problem at Hynish harbour was that it was liable to silting, and Stevenson devised an ingenious method of scouring out the dock. Up to a million gallons of water could be collected in a reservoir above the site, which could be let out through a conduit in a controlled flood to clear the harbour basin and channel of accumulated sand.

13 Skerryvore Lighthouse
19th century.
NL 840263. Situated about 17 km WSW of Tiree.
Harbour and Lightkeepers' Houses, Hynish, Tiree.
NL 9839. Situated near the southernmost tip of Tiree.
Northern Lighthouse Board; Signal Tower Museum, Hynish: Hebridean Trust.

Few visitors will see the magnificent lighthouse of Skerryvore except remotely through binoculars, but the achievement of its construction on a remote wind- and sea-swept reef has an important place in lighthouse history. When Sir Walter Scott visited the

Skerryvore Lighthouse (no. 13).

Hynish, Tiree: dock and pier (no. 13).

TOWNS

The creation of two early burghs illustrates the attempts of the Crown to increase control of the west coast: Tarbert in 1329 and Rothesay in 1401, both taking an important royal castle as the focus; the Rothesay charter uses the term royal burgh for the first time. As early as 1597 Parliament had ordained that burghs be created at Campbeltown, Inverlochy and Stornoway; Campbeltown was founded in the early 17th century, with some of the merchants coming from Rothesay. Fort William has its origin in a military base built at Inverlochy by General Monk in 1655, which was reconstructed on a larger scale in 1690 and takes its name from King William III. One group of

towns is the result of the pioneering efforts of the British Fisheries Society formed in 1786, and the growth of Tobermory, for example, stems from attempts to enable Scottish fishermen to take advantage of the rich herring catches then to be made in the west. Several planned towns are the creation of major land-owners, Bowmore (no. 14) for example, but the most remarkable example of overall vision is that of the 3rd Duke of Argyll in the case of Inveraray (no. 16). Towns of varying sizes are listed in this section in order to highlight particular aspects of their architecture: Bowmore, Campbeltown, Inveraray, Oban, Stornoway and Tobermory (nos 14-19).

Bowmore, Islay: aerial view (no. 14).

Inveraray, (no. 16).

14 Bowmore, Islay.
NR 3159

In 1768 in order to remove the village of Killarow from a position close to Islay House, Daniel Campbell of Shawfield and Islay founded the planned village of Bowmore on the east shore of Loch Indaal, perhaps on the site of an existing pier. The grid plan of the principal section of the village is well illustrated on the air photograph, with Main Street running from the

Bowmore, Islay: Killarow Parish Church (no. 14).

imposing circular parish church to the pier just beyond the bottom of the picture. The more important axial streets are at right angles to Main Street, though Shore Street is curved for obvious reasons. The shape of many of the original feus is shown by the garden walls running back from the main frontages. The distillery founded in 1779 occupies the lower right of the photograph.

The parish church was built by Daniel Campbell in 1767 for the new village; it is circular on plan with a rectangular porch and tower looking down Main Street; the commanding position of the church has been compared to that of Inveraray. The interior retains a pew-layout of the latter part of the last century; there is also a dominant central timber column that supports a complex roof structure. A notable feature is the massive sarcophagus commemorating Lady Ellinor Campbell and Walter Frederick Campbell on the east side of the interior.

15 Campbeltown, Kintyre
NR 7120

The origins of Campbeltown lie in the early 17th century when Archibald Campbell, 7th Earl of Argyll, built a castle on one of the most prominent knolls round the natural harbour (now the site of the Castlehill Church); the attractions of this sheltered bay are clear, and extensive early prehistoric occupation, including mesolithic shell-middens and a series of bronze-age cists with rich gravegoods, has been recorded. The medieval focus was perhaps on the south side of Campbeltown Bay at Kilkerran (NR 728193), where a church dedicated to St Ciaran is recorded by the middle of the 13th century. Today in the Kilkerran Cemetery may be seen an Early Christian cross, a fine cross shaft of 15th-century date, as well as a wide variety of later headstones, the carvings on which reflect the maritime and commercial interests of the later town. The Earl

Campbeltown, Kintyre: Town House (no. 15).

encouraged settlement by Lowlanders in order to stimulate trade and agriculture. In 1700 the town was created a royal burgh, a status it retained until local government reorganisation in 1975. The bustle of Campbeltown today is mainly the result of its growth in the middle of the last century. A view of Main Street on Fair Day dating to 1886 gives an impression of the town at this time. Castlehill Church built between 1778 and 1780 is seen in the background occupying the site of the Earl's castle. The Town House with its elegant octagonal steeple forms the main architectural focus for the painting, with the cross (no. 36) at the centre of the throng. The Town House was built between 1758 and 1760, on the site of an earlier tolbooth, and is one of the most attractive of early buildings representing civic pride in Argyll. The stone spire is about twenty years later than the original building, replacing one in timber. The building that houses the Library and Museum at the middle of Hall Street is of interest not only because of the unusual range of archaeological material on display, but also because of the carved panels on the exterior; there are four panels which illustrate the eight trades that were of particular importance to Campbeltown in past years: coal-mining, fishing, boat-building, flax, learning, distilling and cooperage, and building. One of the unexpected architectural delights of Campbeltown is the Picture House, adjacent to the Museum; known as the Wee Picture House, it was opened in 1913 and is said to be one of the oldest in Scotland. The fairy-tale façade creates an appropriate image for the beginnings of this new medium. The terminal loop of the Campbeltown to Machrihanish Light Railway Company was formerly at the centre of Hall Street opposite the cinema and Library, with the loading terminus on the New Quay; the main depot with carriage-and engine-shed was at Limecraigs. From its foundation Campbeltown had both English- and Gaelic-speaking communities and this is reflected in the number of churches. The Lowland or English-speaking community worshipped between 1706 and about 1778 at the old Lowland Church in Kirk Street

*Campbeltown, Kintyre: on Fair Day
by A MacKinnon, 1886 (no. 15).*

(NR 720203), now a hall; at that time the Castlehill Church shown above was built. The Highland Parish Church, built between 1803 and 1806 for the Gaelic-speaking congregation has both a well-proportioned façade and spacious interior; the steeple is not part of the original design but dates from a re-building in 1884-5.

16 Inveraray, Mid Argyll
NN 0908

The creation of Inveraray as we know it today stems from the determination of Archibald, 3rd Duke of Argyll, who succeeded to the title in 1743. His vision of a new castle and the building of a modern town on a site a little distance away took shape with the advice of the distinguished architect Roger Morris. The Castle is a symmetrical neo-castellated mansion planned by Morris, much of the later interior decoration being to the designs of Robert Mylne for the 5th Duke. The addition of the third (dormer) storey to the main quadrangle and of the conical turrets to the corner towers was the result of the redesigning of the upper part after a fire in 1877. The Castle, for which there is an excellent official guide-book, has many spectacular rooms with collections of tapestries and paintings and displays of weapons. The woodland walk to the summit of Duniquaich offers a panoramic view over the policies and the Town.

There are two important pieces of West Highland sculpture in Inveraray; at the foot of Main Street, the Inveraray cross was moved to its present position as part of the planning of the New Town. Belonging to the Iona School of carving, the cross probably dates to the later 15th century. Like the Campbeltown cross, several figural scenes, including the Crucifix, were removed at the time of the Reformation; the inscription (along one edge and in two lines at the base) reads: 'This is the cross of noble men, namely,

Inveraray Castle, Mid Argyll (no. 16).

Inveraray, Mid Argyll: Courthouse (no. 16).

Inveraray, Mid Argyll: Church (no. 16). Sadly the elegant steeple was taken down in 1941 and the stones were not preserved for subsequent restoration.

Duncanus MacCowan, Patricius, his son, and Mael-Moire, son of Patricius, who caused this cross to be made.'

The second cross, situated in the Castle Gardens (open only on selected weekends), comes originally from Kirkapoll, Tiree. The cross and plinth, which are probably of early 15th century date, are unusual in several respects; it is the best-surviving socket stone from the West Highland series and the inscription, to one side of an attractive leafy design, is carved with unusual clarity. It reads: 'This is the cross of Abbot Fingonius and of his sons Fingonius and Eage'. The crucifixion scene on the front of the cross is surmounted by the figure of St Michael; the hunting scene on the back of the cross, an interlocking design of stag and hunting dogs, forms the central part of the roundel.

The elegant façade on Front Street links several important groups of buildings including the hotel and the Town House; its headland situation means that the unifying arcades provide a dramatic vista of the New Town on its northern approaches. The Main Street has at its focus the twin church of the Highland (Gaelic-speaking) and Lowland (English-speaking) communities; the church was designed by Robert Mylne. The northern part of the church (the Lowland) remains in use for services, while the Highland half is now used as a church hall. The major residential blocks to the south-west of the church are also to designs by Mylne, as are several to the north-east; John Adam was responsible for the Argyll Arms Hotel and the main block between the arcading and Main Street.

In 1747 many aspects of the legal jurisdiction that had been hereditary were abolished, and a system of Circuit Courts established; Inveraray remained, however, an important seat for a court. The Argyll Arms Hotel has its origins in providing a base for the judges themselves as well as the court officials and lawyers. The Courthouse and prison were originally among the buildings designed by John Adam on Front Street; repeated complaints about the inadequacy of the accommodation led to the building of a new Courthouse between 1816-20 to designs by James

Inveraray Castle, Mid Argyll: Garden Bridge (no. 16).

Inveraray, Mid Argyll: Garron Bridge (no. 16).

Inveraray Castle, Mid Argyll: cross-base from Kirkapoll, Tiree (no. 16).

Gillespie Graham. The building and its two attendant prison-blocks are now the headquarters of the department of the District Archivist.

The bridges of Inveraray form such an important part of the architectural setting that they are here listed briefly in chronological order. The Garron Bridge, at the head of the loch, was designed by Roger Morris and built under the direction of John Adam between 1747-9. Adam designed the Garden Bridge, constructed between 1759-61, with a single shallow arch with a span of some 18.3 m. The bridge over the River Aray was designed by Robert Mylne between 1773-6 to replace one that collapsed in 1772. The bridges are among the architectural jewels of Inveraray and help to epitomise its place in 18th century landscape planning.

As tourists in Inveraray today, we owe the preservation and restoration of the castle and town to the combined energies of the 11th Duke of Argyll and to his architect, Ian Lindsay.

Inveraray, Mid Argyll: cross from south-west (no. 16).

Inveraray Castle, Mid Argyll: cross from Kirkapoll, Tiree, hunting scene (no. 16).

Inveraray Castle, Mid Argyll: cross from Kirkapoll, Tiree, crucifixion (no. 16).

Inveraray, Mid Argyll (no. 16).

Inveraray Castle, Mid Argyll:
east front (no. 16).

Duart Castle, Mull: view from east (no. 22).

Dunvegan Castle, Skye (no. 27).

17 Oban, Lorn
NM 8530

Although Oban can proclaim few early buildings, its origins, like those of Campbeltown, go back to the very earliest inhabitants of Scotland, traces of whose remains were found in the course of building programmes in the last century; caves with the occupation debris of some of the earliest hunting communities in Scotland were discovered, together with several cist-burials of bronze-age date, particularly as the northern part of the town was being developed. The medieval stronghold of Dunollie (no. 23), perhaps with its origins in the Dark Ages, underlines the importance of the anchorage, at a time when so much

of west coast communications were seaborne. There was by the early 18th century a prosperous trading-station and by about 1760 a customs house had been established. As illustrated about the middle of the 19th century Oban is shown to have been a neat thriving town with the Free Church and much of George Street already built, with Stafford Street running down to what is now the North Pier.

On 30 June 1880 the Callander and Oban railway was at last complete and Oban was set to become that 'Charing Cross of the Highlands' that it remains today: the railway, together with MacBrayne's steamers, offers holiday-makers access to some of the most spectacular scenery in Scotland. Moreover, from a

Oban, Lorn: view of Oban about 1857 by A Stanley (no. 17).

Oban, Lorn: photograph taken about 1885 by George Washington Wilson (no. 17).

commercial point of view for the fishermen, the railway opened up markets in the south. Even allowing for what is clearly a festive occasion, the Oban of around 1890 as shown in George Washington Wilson's photograph is very different from the illustration of only thirty years before.

Although it may seem unkind to say that Oban has little to offer the architecturally-minded visitor, look up above the modern shop fronts and there are often fine examples of domestic building of later Victorian and early twentieth century styles. The great tower that overlooks the town begun by James Stuart McCaig between 1897 and his death in 1902 is a monument both to himself and to his belief that the masons of Oban should be employed during the lean winter months. Churches of note are the Roman Catholic Cathedral of St Columba on Corran Esplanade; the architect was Sir Giles Gilbert Scott and the building was completed in 1952. Nearby is the attractive church of Christ's Church, Dunollie, built in 1957, designed by the distinguished architect Leslie Grahame MacDougall.

18 Stornoway, Lewis
NB 4232

Stornoway is the principal town in the Western Isles and one of the largest in Argyll and the Isles. A sheltered anchorage on the east coast of Lewis, the site has obviously been of importance for many centuries, though nearly all the buildings to be seen now are of 19th century date or later.

The medieval castle, destroyed by Cromwell's troops in 1654, was the stronghold of the MacLeods who were chiefs in Lewis from the 13th century, but during the 16th century the island passed into the hands of MacKenzie of Kintail and eventually was sold to James Matheson in 1844. The town was already spreading from its early site between North and South Beach and Kenneth Street; Matheson built new houses, improved roads, gas and water supplies, and constructed new quays, which encouraged development of the fishing industry and led to the growth and prosperity of the town. He also built Lews Castle and planted the grounds with a variety of trees and shrubs; the Castle grounds, now open to the public, contain one of the largest areas of deciduous woodland in the Western Isles, and provide a peaceful contrast to the bustle of the town. The Castle is now a College of Further Education.

There are no buildings of outstanding architectural interest, but a number have unusual details and the observant visitor may see a variety of building styles and functions in a stroll through the commercial streets and the quieter parts of town. There are pleasant 19th century frontages on South Beach and above the shops on Cromwell Street, including stone façades and ornate gables. Amity House, the offices of the Pier and Harbour Commission, is a handsome building and nearby on North Beach is a building with loft doors and small round windows under the eaves; this was probably used at one time for drying and storing nets. The former Town Hall on South Beach was built in 1905 in the Scots Baronial style, to designs by John Robertson of Inverness, and is now the location of the new museum, Museum nan Eilean, Steornabhagh, which illustrates the geology and history of the area.

A little further from the centre there is the Nicholson Institute, the only senior secondary school in the

Stornoway, Lewis: Old Town Hall (no. 18).

Stornoway, Lewis: Lews Castle (no. 18).

Tobermory, Mull: aerial view (no. 19).

Western Isles. In Matheson Road there are several houses built by Lord Leverhulme when he was proprietor of the island, and, beyond a vigorous suburban growth, the hospital and an industrial estate, including mills where wool for the Harris tweed is dyed and spun and the completed tweeds are washed and checked.

19 Tobermory, Mull
   NM 5055

Tobermory is of interest not so much because of the excellence of individual buildings, but because it retains to a remarkable degree the townscape of its original purpose as settlement and harbour designed by the British Fisheries Society. The planning and construction of the new settlement to the north-west of the sheltered bay began in 1787 and 1788, the layout of which was dominated by the local topography; the commercial centre was to be close to the shore, while the houses of the workmen were on the terrace above. The various buildings on Main Street have been altered and none of the original houses of the Upper Town survive; a visit should include not only the shops of Main Street, but also the Upper Town from which there are superb views over the Sound of Mull. Only the modern Lego-style fire-station seems incongruous.

Tobermory takes its name from a holy well dedicated to Our Lady (tobar—well, Mhoire—Mary) traditionally situated a little distance from a medieval chapel 400 m west of the town itself. The chapel is now ruinous; within the chapel there is a late medieval tombstone of the Iona school and two other fragmentary slabs.

Tobermory's success was not, however, to lie in fishing, but in more general trade, and its usefulness as a port increased after the opening of the Crinan Canal; indeed in 1844 the British Fisheries Society sold its interest in the town.

CASTLES

The numerous castles of the west coast and islands bear witness both to the relative prosperity of this area during the early Middle Ages, which encouraged their creation, and to the feuding and political uncertainty of later centuries, which prolonged their life into Jacobite times. The west coast was one of the last areas to come under royal authority, a process that began in the 13th century, and many of the castles in the area were built by the major families with some measure of royal assistance. There are so many exciting castles to visit that we have been able to include only a selection of the more important or visually impressive. Among the earliest are castles that show the two aspects of the political make-up of the west; Rothesay (no. 32), on the periphery of our area, is probably a Stewart foundation in the later 12th century; it is a 'castle of enclosure' (a class of castle in which a curtain wall encloses a courtyard), probably with ranges of timber buildings against the wall or free-standing in the interior. Castle Sween on the other hand was built by a west highland magnate, probably the eponymous Suibhne, lord of Knapdale himself, in the later 12th century (no. 21). One of the earliest Campbell castles is that on the island of Innis Chonnell, in Loch Awe (NM 976119); it too was first planned as a simple castle of enclosure. Work at Tarbert Castle (no. 34) in the 13th and early 14th century is the result of direct royal interest in the area. At this time too more developed forms of castles of enclosure with angle towers were being built to take account of new techniques of siege warfare and weapons: Dunstaffnage (no. 25) by the

MacDougalls, and Inverlochy, Lochaber, by the Comyns (NN 120754); it is likely that the drum-towers of Rothesay Castle were added at this time.

A different solution to the building of a well defended residence is the 'hall-house'; stoutly built, and on two or three storeys with a cellar, the main living room or 'hall', and perhaps an upper room. Few are now more than shells, but good detection can show the walls of the original hall-house at Skipness (no. 33), and others of 13th or early 14th century date, can be seen at Ardtornish in Morvern (NM 691426) and Aros on Mull (NM 562449). In Loch Finlaggan on Islay (NR 388681), there are two islands, one of which has the hall, ancillary buildings and chapel appropriate to one of the residences of the MacDonald Lords of the Isles, while the adjacent island was traditionally known as the Council Isle. The beginning of the causeway that formerly linked the two islands can be seen on air photographs.

The tower-houses are perhaps the most striking addition to the west highland landscape, and they are not likely to date to before about the 14th century; Duart (no. 22) belongs to the later 14th century for example. The arrangement of rooms in a simple tower was normally a cellar on the ground floor with the hall above; the upper floors provided sleeping quarters perhaps with a garret. Tower-houses on their own are common throughout lowland Scotland and in the west are found both in isolation and as additions to

Dunderave Castle, Cowal: after restoration.

earlier castles of enclosure in order to provide greater comfort as well as security. This successful style continued to be built for several centuries; Dunderave in Cowal dates to 1596 (NN 143096). Impressive towers include Dunollie (no. 23), probably on the site of an earlier fortification, Kisimul, Barra (no. 29) and Carnassarie (no. 20). Earlier castles were provided with tower-house accommodation as at Skipness (no. 33) and Tarbert (no. 34) probably in the early 16th century. Kilchurn (no. 28) is one of the most important of such castles; founded before the middle of the 15th century by Sir Colin Campbell of Glenorchy, it was in origin one of the earliest tower-houses of the area, but the castle was comprehensively rebuilt between 1690 and 1698 and is thus one of the latest purely defensive houses in the grand manner.

Several tower-houses to which there is only limited or indeed no public access, or castles which have few architectural details, may nonetheless be appreciated from a distance or from the immediate exterior: these include Breachacha on Coll (NM 159539), a tower with an additional curtain wall both dating to about 1430-50; Kinlochaline in Morvern (NM 697476); and Moy, Mull (NM 616247)–all three castles of branches of the MacLean family; Gylen on Kerrera (NM 805264), a magnificent tower with an unusual decorated upper window, completed by Duncan MacDougall in 1582; Castle Stalker, a mid 16th century tower of the Stewarts of Appin (NM 920473) (a fine restored castle on an island, open by appointment); and Barcaldine, an early 17th century tower of Campbell of Glenorchy (also open by appointment). The two castles at Breachacha illustrate the architectural aspirations of the west Highland chief at three distinct periods and their location underlines the importance of a safe anchorage for the chieftain's boats. The tower-house belongs to the 15th century and the new mansion dates to 1750 with further additions of a century later (NM 159539). Breachacha New Castle was originally a square block of three storeys built about 140 m to the NW of the medieval castle by Hector MacLean, the Laird of Coll. Johnson and Boswell were among his early guests staying at the mansion in October 1773; Johnson was cutting in his comments on the new work, remarking that 'there was nothing becoming a Chief about it: it was a mere tradesman's box'. Boswell perhaps mellow as a result of the rigours of their sea voyage found it 'a neat new-built gentleman's house with four rooms on a floor, three storeys and garrets'. The travellers visited the medieval castle, noting that part of it was still in use as a family prison. About a century later the mansion was refurbished by the addition of a fourth storey and more elaborate side-pavilions. In the southern approaches to the area mention may also be made of Carrick Castle, Cowal (NS 194944) and Saddell Castle in Kintyre (NR 789315), which was built between 1508 and 1512 for the Bishop of Argyll.

One of the rare representations of a medieval castle appears on the tomb of Alexander MacLeod in St Clement's Church, Rodel, on Harris (no. 49); the tomb is known to date to 1528 but it is possible that the model for this part of the carving is Irish rather than Scottish. The castle has two towers and battlements with stepped crenellations in a particular Irish form. The smaller tower has a raised drawbridge to which there is access up side steps–an arrangement comparable to that at Dunstaffnage (no. 25).

Breachacha Castle, Coll.

New Breachacha Castle, Coll.

Castle Stalker, Lorn.

20 Carnassarie Castle, Mid Argyll

c AD 1560-1570

NM 839008. Situated on the west side of the A 816 Lochgilphead to Oban road, just north of Kilmartin.

HBM (SDD).

This impressive tower-house rises from a ridge that dominates the upper part of the Kilmartin Valley. The tower was built on the site of an earlier castle, and there may even be the remains of a small dun on the

Carnassarie Castle, Mid Argyll (no. 20).

now grass-covered knoll immediately to the north-east. One of the latest of the tower-houses, it was built by a famous churchman John Carswell; he was superintendent of Argyll and the Isles in the Reformed Church from 1562 and was granted the bishopric of the Isles in 1567. Carswell was an influential figure in spreading the ideals of the Reformed religion in Argyll in the middle of the 16th century, and he published a Gaelic translation of the *Book of Common Order* or *Knox's Liturgy* in 1567; the first book to be printed in Gaelic, it contained the doctrines of the Presbyterian faith. The castle was built in the later 1560s under the patronage of the Earl of Argyll. The main hall was in the western wing of the castle, above the kitchen and storerooms, and the withdrawing room was on the same level on the first floor of the tower. This *en suite* arrangement is of some importance as it is thought to be transitional between castles and later mansion-houses, with the various rooms laid out in a horizontal rather than a vertical manner as in a traditional tower-house. The main part of the tower is on five storeys with basal cellarage; the first-floor withdrawing room has a magnificent fireplace with finely carved surround and similar crisp detail round the doorways. The upper floors do not survive, but it is worth climbing to the upper parapet because there is a superb view down the valley. Only the shell of the western portion of the castle survives, but attractive outer string-mouldings still remain, as well as a rich provision of gun-loops and shot-holes.

The inscribed panel above the doorway reads in Gaelic *Dia le ua nduibhne* translated as 'God be with O Duibhne'; O Duibhne is one of the styles of the chief of the Campbells, though one that was not current in the 1560s, and its use here suggests a conscious antiquarianism on Carswell's part. The heraldic panel is a combination of those of Campbell of Argyll and the royal arms of Scotland, probably indicating the marriage of Archibald 5th Earl of Argyll and Jean, a daughter of James V; the panel thus underlines Carswell's allegiance to the earl.

21 Castle Sween, Mid Argyll

Late 12th–15th century AD.
NR 712788. Situated on the east side of Loch Sween about 17 km south-west of Bellanoch.
HBM (SDD).

The imposing castle stands on a rocky ridge close to the shore of Loch Sween within the policies of the Castle Sween Caravan Park. The castle is remarkable both for the state of preservation of the main walls and for the sophistication of the original construction. On plan it is a quadrangular castle of enclosure with projecting buttresses at the angles and at the centre of each of the walls; although primarily for defensive strength, the buttresses also give the castle a more pleasing exterior than many of the bare boxes of the west highland castles of enceinte. The gateway is in the south wall where the wall has been made thicker, not only to provide additional defence at door level, but also to make possible a platform above the door. Within the interior of this late 12th century castle, timber ranges round the wall would have provided accommodation, and the lines of support for internal floors and roofing are clearly visible. There is a well in the north-east angle. The MacMillan Tower outside the north-east angle is of later, probably 15th century date; the basement floor contains kitchen and bakehouse oven with on upper floors, the hall, the lord's apartment and bedrooms. The unadorned narrow windows with pointed arches and simple inner splays are almost the only surviving architectural features of the tower. The round tower at the north-west angle, which appears to be of similar date, contained a prison and has a complex drain arrangement.

Little is known of the castle's history but it was probably besieged by Robert Bruce during his campaigns in the west. Some impression of the more civilised aspects of life in the castle is provided by the description of the meeting between John, Lord of the Isles and Earl Douglas in 1483, probably at Castle Sween; the former received 'right great gifts' of clothes, wine, silk, English cloth and silver, and offered Earl Douglas a present of mantles. The castle became ruinous after attack by Colkitto in 1647.

Castle Sween, Mid Argyll (no. 21).

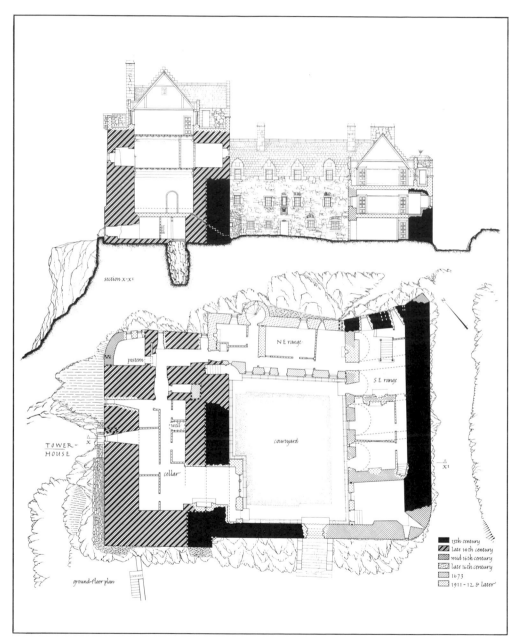

section x-x¹

TOWER-
HOUSE

postern

well

cellar

courtyard

N E range

S E range

ground-floor plan

- 13th century
- late 14th century
- mid 16th century
- late 16th century
- 1673
- 1911-12 & later

22* Duart Castle, Mull

13th to 17th centuries AD.
NM 748353. Signposted on the A 849 near the
eastern tip of Mull.

The outstanding location of Duart Castle, dominating
the southern approach to the Sound of Mull and
visible by every traveller to Mull and the southern
Hebrides, has helped to make Duart one of the classic
residences of the Highland chieftain. There is an
excellent guidebook to the castle describing its history
and the contents of the main rooms; here we shall
describe briefly the main architectural features, some
of which were masked by the extensive renovations of
1911-12 by Colonel Sir Fitzroy MacLean, 26th Chief of
the Clan MacLean.

The original fortification was a simple castle of
enclosure probably rectangular on plan measuring
about 21.5 m by 19.7 m internally; today the only
portions of this work are on the south-east section of
the curtain wall and the western corner of the present
courtyard. This was probably a MacDougall castle
dating to about the 13th century. The main portion of
the castle, the tower-house, is of late 14th century date
by which time it was already in MacLean hands; the
tower-house abuts the earlier work using the western
corner of the earlier castle, and employing its walls as a
stoutly defended courtyard. The unusually massive
tower-house has four principal floors: cellars at the
bottom, a first-floor hall (now the Banqueting Hall),
the second floor (with the present Ante-Room and
State Bedroom); the upper floors now house the Scout
Exhibition.

The MacLean estates were lost to the family in the
1670s, though the castle continued to play an
important part in the military affairs of the west. The
final chapter of the castle's history begins in 1911 with
the purchase of the castle by Sir Fitzroy MacLean and
the initiation of the programme of restoration that has

preserved the fabric, as well as adding features such as the Sea Room, more appropriate to the 20th century.

---

23 Dunollie Castle, Lorn

c 15th century AD.
NM 852314. On the road to Ganavan just to the north-west of Oban.

This tower-house occupies a conspicuous position on the summit of a rocky ridge to the north of Oban; the lands of Dunollie have one of the longest recorded histories in the west, for in 698 a fortress here was captured and destroyed by the Irish enemies of the

Dunollie Castle, Lorn (no. 23).

kings of Dalriada, but the date of the building of the castle as the seat of the MacDougalls has been a matter of debate. It is, however, most likely that it takes its place within the series of broadly 15th century towers, with the courtyard wall of similar and later date. The tower has four main storeys, with a cellar beneath two simple rooms reached by stairs in the south angle. An unusual feature of the cellar is the impression left by the wicker-work used to support the roof during construction, a technique more common in Ireland than in Scotland. A stair leads from the entrance passage to the first floor, a similar right-angled stair from the first- to the second-floor hall, and a turnpike stair from there to the upper levels.

In 1715 the chief of the clan MacDougall was forfeited, but the lands were later restored to his son and the more modern residence, Dunollie House (NM 853315), was built in 1746.

---

24 Dun Scaich, Skye

Medieval period.
NG 595120. Leave the A 851 at either Ostaig or a little south of Isle Ornsay and follow the narrow winding road to Tarskavaig. Dun Scaich can be seen from the road about 2 km north of Tarskavaig, where the road runs close to the shore. Walk along the north side of the bay.

Dun Scaich or Dun Scaith is said to have been built in a single night by the fairies or by a witch. It was to this fortress that the hero Cuchulainn came for instruction in the arts of war by the warrior Queen Scathach according to legend. It is described as being surrounded by seven ramparts crowned by iron palisades and protected by a pit full of snakes and beaked toads! Whatever its traditional origin, the castle was used in late medieval times by the MacDonalds of Sleat.

The most impressive aspect of Dun Scaich is now its landward side, where the wall stands in places to a height of 5 m. It is built upon a rock with precipitous sides, and approached by a causeway, partly natural, which leads to a bridge over a gully in the rock. The floor of the bridge is now missing. Beyond this a flight of steps climbs between walls to the entrance, to the left of which the wall stands to a considerable height; in the corner to the right there are the remains of a room incorporating a garderobe. The whole of the top of the rock was originally enclosed by a wall on all but the east side. Turf covered wall-bases or foundations show where some interior buildings stood. The break in the wall on the south side was probably a sea-gate.

In the early 17th century the MacDonalds moved to Duntulm, in Trotternish (no. 26) but later returned to Sleat, to their new residence at Armadale (no. 1).

Dunstaffnage Chapel, Lorn: north wall (no. 25).

25* Dunstaffnage Castle and Chapel, Lorn

13th–16th centuries AD.
NM 882344 and NM 880344. Signposted at Dunbeg on the A 85 between Oban and Connel. HBM (SDD).

This magnificent castle occupies the summit of an isolated rock stack at the head of Loch Etive, with the sheltered anchorage of Dunstaffnage Bay to the east. The castle was founded by the MacDougall family, Lords of Lorn, either Duncan MacDougall, who founded the priory of Ardchattan, or his son Ewen, and it dates in origin to the middle of the 13th century. The ground plan is largely determined by the quadrangular shape of the top of the rock stack; the walls are massive, rising from the conglomerate stack to form a castle of enclosure but with stout slightly projecting angle towers at the north and west corners and with an entrance tower at the east angle. Doubtless much of the accommodation within the castle would have been in stone and timber ranges against the curtain walls particularly on the north-west; rather grander accommodation, possibly including a first-floor hall, is implied by the architectural details of the east side, with the blocked windows of these rooms still visible from the outside. The castle was captured from the MacDougalls by Robert Bruce in 1309 and for some years it remained in royal hands. After several other holders in the 14th and 15th centuries the castle was, in 1470, granted to Colin, 1st Earl of Argyll; in 1502 the custody of the castle was vested by the then earl in his cousin, who became known as the Captain of Dunstaffnage. Today the castle belongs to the Duke of Argyll, with the hereditary Captain as the keeper of the castle with right of residence, though the guardianship of the castle is now vested in the Secretary of State for Scotland.

It is a measure of the success of the original concept that the castle has, except at the entrance tower, been so little altered. In the late 15th or early 16th century

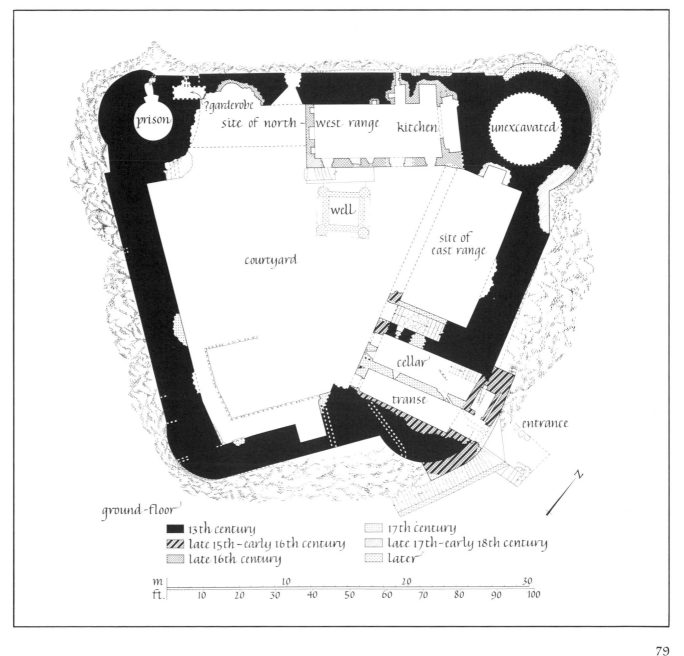

prison

?garderobe

site of north-west range

kitchen

unexcavated

well

site of
east range

courtyard

cellar

transe

entrance

ground-floor

	13th century		17th century
	late 15th–early 16th century		late 17th–early 18th century
	late 16th century		later

m   10   20   30
ft.   10   20   30   40   50   60   70   80   90   100

Dunstaffnage Castle, Lorn (no. 25).

the entrance was re-arranged with the rebuilding of part of the east tower; access was across a wooden drawbridge at the head of angled steps leading from the base of the rock stack. The upper part of the gateway is probably of late 16th century date. Further alterations continued till 1810 largely to improve the domestic arrangements of the north-west range and the gate-tower, though work to allow the greater use of firearms in the defence of the castle was also undertaken.

The chapel situated about 150 m WSW of the castle was built in the second quarter of the 13th century,

with the burial-aisle of the Campbells of Dunstaffnage continuing the line of building at the east end. The chapel is of simple rectangular plan, but the detail of the mouldings of the windows is of an intricacy and quality remarkable in the west of Scotland at this time. The three pairs of windows of the chancel have been the main areas of such decoration with dog-tooth ornament on the outside; the paired windows on the north and south sides of the chancel are particularly fine examples of Gothic embellishment. The architectural style of the chapel has been compared to contemporary work at the Nunnery on Iona (no. 43) and the parish church at Killean (no. 46).

26 Duntulm Castle, Skye
Medieval period and 17th century AD.
NG 409743. Signposted on the A 855 at the north end of Trotternish.

There has probably been a defensive structure on the site of the castle at Duntulm for centuries, but the ruined buildings which now stand there have obliterated any traces of an earlier fortress. The lands of Trotternish were the subject of rival claims by the MacLeods of Dunvegan and the MacDonalds of Sleat, and it was probably to consolidate their possession that the MacDonalds moved to Duntulm from Dun Scaich (no. 24) in the early 17th century. King James V visited the castle in 1540 and is said to have been favourably impressed by its strength and hospitality, but in the early 17th century Sir Donald MacDonald improved it as a dwelling. It was abandoned about 1730 when the family went to live at Monkstadt, a little further south.

The castle stands on a crag, with cliffs and steep slopes on three sides and a dry ditch on the south. The earliest surviving structure is a rectangular building facing the ditch, with a wall enclosing the summit of the rock. Very little of this earliest building remains, though there is a barrel-vaulted basement at the south west corner. The main entrance was across the ditch, but there is also a sea-gate in the wall on the opposite side of the courtyard. A small tower with a vaulted room on the ground floor was added in the 17th century and parts of this tower still stand to the full height. Another building was added in the north-west corner of the courtyard.

Among those who died in the dungeon here was Hugh MacDonald, cousin of Donald Gorm, the 8th chief. He had plotted to supplant Donald Gorm but the plan miscarried and, after hiding in Dun an Sticir, North Uist (no. 57) for some time, Hugh was captured and left in the dungeon at Duntulm with a plate of salt beef and an empty pitcher.

27* Dunvegan Castle, Skye
14th–19th century AD.
NG 247490. Signposted off the A 850 just north of Dunvegan village.

Dunvegan Castle, the ancient seat of the MacLeods of Dunvegan and Harris, stands on a rock on the east shore of Loch Dunvegan, protected from the landward side by a deep gully. The oldest part is the keep, dating probably to the 14th century, a four-storey tower similar to those at Kisimul (no. 29), Caisteal Uisdein and Castle Maol, and used as a dwelling as well as a defensive structure. As at Kisimul the original plan included a wall enclosing a courtyard, with the only entrance through the sea-gate. There is a well in the courtyard which belongs to this period. The tower has a small wing on the north-west gable. The barrel-vaulted room at the base of the tower was originally a cellar, but later became the kitchen. At the same level in the wing is the dungeon, entered from the floor above by a trap door. The hall occupies the first floor of the tower.

In the 16th century Alasdair Crotach, whose elaborate tomb is in the church at Rodel (no. 49), built the 'Fairy Tower' within the south-east angle of the wall, providing further accommodation. In the 17th century the space between the two towers was built over by Rory Mor; this house included a spacious dining-room and a library. By the late 17th century, the tower had fallen into disuse, and a wing was built onto the Fairy Tower.

Late in the 18th century, a further building was added, to the north-west of the tower, a barracks to hold men of the 2nd Battalion Black Watch which the General, the 23rd Chief of the Clan MacLeod, was raising locally. Part of this now houses an exhibition including material about Clan MacLeod, local history, and St Kilda (no. 7), which belonged to the family for several centuries. Amongst the items on view are the famous

'Fairy Flag', a silken banner of Eastern origin, said to have been given to one of the chiefs by a fairy and to provide magical protection for the clan when waved; and the Dunvegan Cup, a beaker of bog oak with mountings of silver and precious stones, and an inscription which dates from the later 15th century. The imposing front entrance was built early in the 19th century, and access was then possible from the landward side across a bridge. An old armorial panel was built into the porch. The tower was restored and modernised in the mid 19th century, when other alterations were made and the whole castle finished in the 'Baronial' style.

Kilchurn Castle, Lorn (no.28).

15th–17th century AD.
NN 132276. Signposted on the A 85 Dalmally to Taynuilt road 2 km WNW of Dalmally.
HBM (SDD).

At the north-eastern end of Loch Awe the impressive ruin of Kilchurn Castle is situated on a small rocky outcrop almost surrounded by the waters of the loch. Loch Awe was clearly an important route in historical times, as probably in the prehistoric period, and there are several castles along it including Fincharn (NM 898043) and Innis Chonnell (NM 976119), but the strategic importance of Kilchurn to the Campbells of Glenorchy with estates both in Loch Awe and Perthshire was considerable. The surviving remains belong to two distinct schemes of construction: a tower-house built in the middle of the 15th century by Sir Colin Campbell of Glenorchy; and the addition of ranges of barracks within a defensive scheme that had corner towers built by John, 1st Earl of Breadalbane in the last decade of the 17th century.

The tower-house, now an empty shell, has five storeys, the lowest of which is a vaulted cellar, with what was doubtless a prison on its south-east side. The main apartment was the first-floor hall, probably entered from a doorway into the courtyard by means of a wooden stair; there is also a narrow stair from the cellar. The separate staircases to the upper floors are within the angles of the walls.

One of the most dramatic features of the castle as it survives today are the dominant circular angle towers on the north and south flanks; these are the main architectural embellishments of the late 17th century barrack ranges. The barracks played their part intermittently in the military politics of the next sixty years, but the castle was struck by lightning in the 1760s and was not subsequently refurbished. The energies of the Earl of Breadalbane were devoted to his castle and estates at Taymouth in Perthshire.

29* Kisimul Castle, Barra
13th–17th century AD.
NL 665979. An islet in Castle Bay.

Kisimul Castle instantly impresses the visitor entering Castle Bay by ferry; the fortress rises forbiddingly from its rock in the sea and, even before restoration, was fairly well preserved. It was for four centuries the stronghold of the MacNeils, who held Barra from the Lord of the Isles from the early 15th century.

The oldest part of the building is the tower, which, together with most of the curtain wall, may be ascribed to the early 15th century, and was the primary dwelling, consisting of three storeys: a cellar

Kisimul Castle, Barra (no. 29).

with living accommodation over, the upper of the two rooms being the hall. Staircases within the thick walls connect these two rooms and the parapet above, the cellar being entered from the courtyard, and entrance to the tower itself by a bridge from the parapet walk on the curtain wall. The parapet and the two upper rooms are provided with garderobes. The parapet walls of both tower and curtain wall were raised by several feet some time after the original building, and this necessitated the reorganisation of the walks on the tower and the construction of a timber walk on the curtain wall. Other buildings ranged against this wall surround an open courtyard. Opposite the keep is a smaller tower with a curved internal wall; the ground floor was used as a prison and could be entered only by a hatch from the floor above. The hall was probably built at the same time as the curtain wall and small tower, and a building traditionally identified as a chapel. The hall was originally a single-storey building, but in the 17th century it was raised, and a two-storey building was added at the south-west end, covering the well and blocking the postern gate.

Not long after these buildings were completed, others were erected: the kitchen, adjacent to the main tower, the Tanist (or heir's) house, and the Gokman's (watchman's) house. The latter was later enlarged in a way that blocked off the original main gate of the Castle, and a new entrance was created beside the corner of the tower.

At one time there was also a secondary structure outside the tower, beside the boat-landing, but this, together with the Tanist house, the Gokman's house and part of the curtain wall were removed in the 19th century to provide ballast for the herring fleets.

Despite its strong defensive position, the castle is known to have been taken once, during a family disagreement in the 17th century, by twenty men. Major restoration by the late R L MacNeil of Barra was completed in 1970.

30 Knock Castle or Castle Camus, Sleat, Skye

Medieval period.

NG 671087. This is approached by following the track to Knock House, just north of Knock Bay. Pass between the house and farm buildings and at the end of the track cross a bridge on the left. Turn immediately to the right and follow a rough path beside the burn.

This castle, a residence of the MacDonalds of Sleat, stands on a low knoll, protected by crags on the south and west sides, but is approached without much difficulty from the north. The west wall and parts of the south wall stand to a height of at least two storeys but the remainder of the walls are mostly ruinous and turf covered. The site is of architectural interest, however, as it may be the only example of a 'hall-house' to be seen in Skye and the Outer Hebrides.

Mingary Castle, Lochaber: aerial view (no. 31).

31 Mingary Castle, Lochaber

13th–18th century AD.

NM 502631. Situated on the shore beyond Mingary 1.5 km south-east of Kilchoan.

This castle has one of the most impressive locations of all those in the west, visible from and offering extensive panoramas over Mull and Morvern, although it has been stressed that the castle lacks a good anchorage nearby; it stands on an isolated rock stack and, like other 13th century castles of enclosure, it owes its plan to the shape of its natural foundation. The simple multi-angular curtain wall, up to 3 m thick at the base and standing to a height of 14 m, is still remarkably intact, but there are now no traces of the internal buildings of the original construction; the ranges on the north, west and south-east walls are of 17th and 18th century date. There are thus few 13th century architectural details, but it is worth looking out for the lancet windows in the north curtain wall and the original battlements, parts of which were incorporated within a late 16th century rebuilding, and the pit-prison set within the west wall. The main entrance was in the north-west angle, and access to it must have been made possible by the provision of a wooden drawbridge spanning the deep rock-cut ditch. The postern entrance or sea-gate in the south wall is now considered to be a late 16th century feature, rather than being part of the original construction.

The castle had an eventful history suffering many attacks and a famous siege in 1644, and it says much for the skills of the original builders that so much of the fabric remains today.

Castle Tioram at the head of Loch Moidart (NM 662724) has a rather similar plan to that of Mingary and rises from a steep sea-girt rock. A tower-house, built in the south-west angle of the original castle of enclosure, has impressive angle turrets. Intending visitors should, however, beware of the advancing tide.

32* Rothesay Castle, Bute

12th–16th century AD.
NS 087645. In the centre of Rothesay; signposted.
HBM (SDD).

This magnificent castle, set on an area of no immediately obvious defensive potential, is one of the best preserved early castles in Scotland; Rothesay Bay is an anchorage of some importance, and proximity to the bay has clearly influenced the siting of the castle. Unlike those castles whose shape was largely dictated by local topography, the builders at Rothesay were free to choose the ground plan, and the result is an almost circular castle of enclosure just over 40 m in diameter with an entrance to the north and a postern on the western flank. The wall is about 2.5 m thick. It is currently suggested that the date of the original castle is in the third quarter of the 12th century. In 1230 the castle was besieged and captured by the Norsemen who had to withstand molten lead and pitch which was poured from the battlements; and it fell again to the Norsemen in 1263 during King Hakon's campaign which culminated in the Battle of Largs.

Rothesay Castle, Bute: aerial view (no. 32).

The four great drum towers appear to have been added to the castle in the later 13th or early 14th century and the wall head of the enclosing wall was remodelled at this time, thus encapsulating some of the original machicolation, and if the moat were not first scarped at this stage it was certainly reshaped to a more rectilinear plan in order to accommodate the towers. It is possible, however, that the moat may belong to a period of building earlier than the castle of enclosure.

The final phase of this spectacular castle is the building of an impressive gatehouse; begun in the reign of James IV, who in 1498 granted to Ninian Stewart the hereditary keepership of the castle, it was completed by James V after 1541. The gatehouse gives an impression of the higher standards of comfort expected in royal residences with the great hall on the first floor with a fireplace and spacious window seating; on the second floor were the private rooms and perhaps an oratory. In the interior of the castle there is a chapel, dedicated to St Michael, which is probably contemporary with this period.

Restoration of the castle was undertaken between 1872 and 1879 by the 3rd Marquess of Bute, and the hereditary keepership of the castle remains vested in the Stuart family although it was formally placed in the guardianship of the State in 1951.

Rothesay Castle, Bute: drum tower (no. 32).

Rothesay Castle, Bute: gate tower (no. 32).

33 Skipness Castle and Kilbrannan Chapel, Kintyre

13th–16th century AD.

NR 908577 and NR 901575. To the east of Skipness village at the end of the B 8001.

HBM (SDD).

The magnificent castle of Skipness has a sequence of construction from the first half of the 13th century until it was abandoned at the end of the 17th century. It was first mentioned in 1261 when it was held by Dugald, son of Sween, presumably on behalf of the MacDonald chiefs; it remained in MacDonald hands until 1493 with the final forfeiture of John, Lord of the Isles, and subsequently was granted to the 2nd Earl of Argyll. The two earliest parts of the castle, a hall-house and separate chapel, were incorporated within the curtain wall of a castle of enceinte in the late 13th or early 14th century, the hall-house at the north-west corner and the chapel forming part of the inner wall on the south. The walls of the great courtyard castle survive almost to their original height with a complex gatehouse on the south wall which has a portcullis

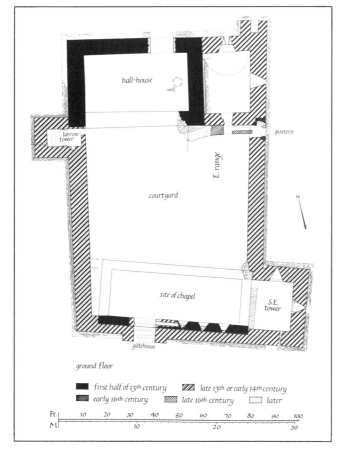

ground floor

- ■ first half of 13th century
- ▨ late 13th or early 14th century
- ▨ early 16th century
- ▨ late 16th century
- ☐ later

Skipness Castle, Kintyre: tower-house from south-west (no. 33).

*Skipness Castle, Kintyre: general
view from north-west (no. 33).*

*Skipness Castle, Kintyre: general
view from south-west (no. 33).*

*Kilbrannan Chapel, Skipness,
Kintyre: interior from north-east
(no. 33).*

chamber above it; on the west wall there is a projecting latrine tower. The building of the three upper floors at the north-east corner of the castle are of rather later date probably at the beginning of the 16th century.

The chapel, dedicated to St Brendan, is situated 320 m south-east of the castle; it dates from the same period as the reconstruction of the castle in the late 13th or early 14th century, at which time an earlier chapel was incorporated within the castle itself and its ecclesiastical use forgotten. The new chapel is a long building with the nave at the west end and the chancel to the east; the side-walls and gables survive almost intact. The window- and door-mouldings are almost complete and, though plain or with simple decoration are described as of Anglo-Scottish First Pointed style.

34 Tarbert Castle, Kintyre

13th–16th century AD.

NR 867686. The castle is approached up a steep path from the south quay at Tarbert just beyond the bookshop; signposted.

The remains of Tarbert Castle are not, perhaps, remarkable in themselves, but the individual elements are unusual, and the view from the castle over the harbour is a panoramic one. The position is of some importance commanding the porterage from Tarbert to West Loch Tarbert, enshrined in one of the earliest memories of Scottish history of many a schoolboy as the place where Magnus Barelegs dragged his vessel across the isthmus to claim Kintyre in about 1098. This was symbolically repeated by Robert Bruce in the period after the Battle of Bannockburn, when the king is known to have taken possession of the castle. The castle occupies the summit of a flattish-topped rocky ridge and comprises three main parts; the most prominent, the tower-house, is the most recent, dating to about AD 1500.

The earliest castle occupied the highest part of the ridge to the south-west of the tower and is a simple rectangular enclosure some 38 m by 33 m internally. Only the lowest courses now survive (and these are best seen in winter or spring when the vegetation is low); they indicate a castle with four ranges of buildings with an entrance on the north-east flank. The plan of the castle may be paralleled by royal castles in the east of Scotland and by analogy it has been suggested, in the absence of documentary evidence, that the castle results from a royal expedition to Kintyre in the early 13th century.

The lower portion of the summit area to the north-east was enclosed by a wall about a century later, appreciably increasing the size of the castle; little survives of this phase except parts of two circular projecting towers on the north-east flank. It is likely that this work dates to the period when Robert took the castle intending it to be a power-base in the area. It is hard to believe this from the surviving remains, but the area enclosed by the wall could have held many timber buildings; building accounts for 1325-6 show that the work on the castle included not only the walls, but also the construction of a hall with clay and sand walls, timber uprights and a thatched roof. From about 1329 Tarbert was established as a royal burgh, perhaps originally situated in the area just to the south-west of the castle.

The castle was the scene of another royal visit in 1494, and James IV was probably responsible for initiating the building of the tower-house, of which only the cellar and the north-east and north-west walls still remain.

Kilbrannan Chapel, Skipness, Kintyre: east end (no. 33).

6

ECCLESIASTICAL MONUMENTS

Early Christian and medieval monuments

The monasteries and oratories of the first Christian monks and missionaries have left few traces, for they were usually built of wood. The *scriptorium* would have been one of the most important places within the monastery, and the keeping of annals (a tally of some of the most important events of the year) and the writing of the lives of saints, alongside the transcription of the gospels and liturgical books, allowed the west of Scotland to enter the historical record for the first time. We know that there were sieges at Dunadd in 683 and 736 for example, but more importantly, from the *Life of Columba* we can create a picture of the routine of the monastic community of Iona and infer something of the buildings there. The early monastery was enclosed within an earthwork bank, parts of which can still be seen; the monastic complex consisted of the various cells of the community, the church and *scriptorium*. Adamnan also tells us something of the agricultural work of the monks, and it is likely that their fields were on the sandy grasslands on the west coast of the island. By the 8th century the monastery was part of a wide net-work of artistic and intellectual communities in touch with one another from Northumbria and Pictland in the east to Ireland in the west; the most remarkable achievements of this formative period of Christian expression are the great crosses that were carved on Iona in the 8th and 9th centuries. The *scriptorium* of the monastery is sometimes put forward

Eilean Munde, Loch Leven, Lochaber: commemorative slab showing Duncan McKenzie dismounting and killing a dragoon at the battle of Prestonpans (1745).

as that in which the Book of Kells was transcribed and illustrated.

Columba's visit to the Pictish king Bridei is one of the most dramatic passages in Adamnan's *Life* of the saint, and, theatrical and traditional as the passages may be, they serve to remind us that the territory north of Ardnamurchan was, nominally at least, under Pictish control. Several of the distinctive carved stones erected by Picts have been found in the northern part of our area, including that at Clach Ard, Tote, Skye (no. 52), and they are of broadly 7th century date.

The symbols include representations of animals and of everyday objects such as combs and mirrors, but others are curvilinear and geometrical designs which cannot be readily understood; these have outlandish, but descriptive, modern names such as 'crescent and V-rod', 'double disc and Z-rod' and 'serpent and Z-rod'. Few stones are still in position, or near their original position, but that at Clach Ard, Tote, Skye (no. 52) is a fine example, and there is another at Dunvegan Castle (no. 27), which bears crescent and double disc symbols. Stones which have been moved for safety to NMAS include that from Fiskavaig, Loch Bracadale, Skye, with double disc and Z-rod and crescent and V-rod symbols, and one from Benbecula, with rectangular and circular motifs. On Raasay there is a fine slab, now preserved near Raasay House, at NG 546367, with a cross in a rectilinear handled frame sometimes called a 'flabellum', with a 'broken-sword' or 'tuning-fork' symbol and a crescent and V-rod. A similar cross is incised on rock face near the shore at Churchton Bay (NG 545363). On the remote island of Pabbay (NL 607874), there is a stone with a 'flower' symbol as well as a crescent and V-rod and a cross. Symbol stones have a dense distribution in the main areas of Pictland in eastern Sutherland, Aberdeenshire and Angus for example; their sparse scatter in the west is an indication of how tenuous was the authority of the Pictish kings over the northern part of the western seaboard.

Apart from important centres such as Iona, remote hermitages as places of meditation and prayer played an important part in the early church. Islands such as Eilean Mor, at the mouth of Loch Sween (NR 666752) provided an ideal setting: a cave here is said to have been used by St Abban as a retreat, and there are two crosses incised on the east wall. A medieval chapel underlines the holiness of the island (HBM, SDD). Indeed the foundation of the Benedictine abbey on Iona and the siting of the cathedral of the medieval diocese of Argyll on the island of Lismore illustrate the importance of the sanctity with which Early Christian sites were endowed in later times. Many of the medieval foundations result from the patronage of the major families–the MacDougalls and the MacDonald Lords of the Isles. The monastery at Saddell, in Kintyre, for example, was founded either by Somerled or his son Reginald after the middle of the 12th century; this was a Cistercian house stemming from Mellifont in Co. Louth. The Benedictine abbey of Iona was founded around 1200, and building continued for several decades. The Nunnery too, dating to about 1220, made use of Irish masons, and the influence of contemporary Irish decoration has been identified in the major ecclesiastical buildings of this time. A monastery founded by Duncan MacDougall about 1230 at Ardchattan on Loch Etive now forms the core of a mansion house, and, although on plan much of the original arrangement can be worked out, the site is chiefly of interest for the collection of carved stones

(NM 971349). The importance of Iona cannot be underestimated as a source of the decorative motifs and architectural design of several of the more elaborate churches of the 13th century, particularly Killean (no. 46) and Dunstaffnage (no. 25). Several simple churches of this period have also been included, although little architectural detail may now be visible: Inchkenneth (no. 42) and Teampull na Trionaid, Carinish, North Uist (no. 37). Kilbrannan Chapel, Skipness (no. 33) is rather later. The siting of the cathedral for the diocese of Argyll on Lismore (no. 47), doubtless because of its earlier foundation, created considerable inconvenience, and the building, which is of early 14th century date, has little architectural embellishment.

The island of Oronsay was chosen for a priory of Augustinian canons founded by John I, Lord of the Isles in the second quarter of the 14th century, but much of the present work is of late 14th to early 15th century date (no. 48). Important renovations were undertaken later in that century when the priory became an important centre for stone carving. Much of the ecclesiastical architecture of the west is thus associated with the important monastic centres like Iona, Ardchattan and Oronsay, and the seats of secular power as at Dunstaffnage. One of the best preserved of later medieval churches is that of St Clement's, Rodel, Harris (no. 49), founded about 1520 and containing one of the most remarkable pieces of late medieval sculpture–the tomb of Alexander MacLeod, dating to 1528.

Late medieval crosses and graveslabs

In the late medieval period a distinctive art style flourished throughout the area of our volume; the visitor today sees the great crosses and intricately designed graveslabs, sometimes grouped in small collections as at Saddell or Kilberry, sometimes taken into a church for safety as at Lochaline, but often open to the elements in the burial-ground. It is worth

Canna: east face of cross.

stressing that the Early Christian stones and the West Highland slabs and crosses, although they may be collected into the same lapidarium as at Iona and Kilmory, or within the same graveyard as at Kilmartin, belong to two distinct periods of carving with no continuity of craft traditions. This double flowering of stone carving of such a high order is one of the most striking features of the heritage of Argyll and the Western Isles. Where appropriate in describing a church or chapel, we have made mention of some of the many slabs that may be seen either in or around it. They have recently been studied in detail, and the various schools of carving outlined in the definitive volume by Dr KA Steer and Dr JWM Bannerman, *Late Medieval Monumental Sculpture in the West Highlands*, have been followed here. Where there is an inscription on a stone, usually in Latin, a translation is given following that of Steer and Bannerman. The crosses and graveslabs offer a fascinating thread to the exploration of Argyll and the Isles, the artistic stability of the schools of carving illustrating the political cohesion of the area. There are many frankly pedestrian pieces, but we have tried to choose examples that underline the skills of the carvers rather than the production-line nature of some of the results.

The Iona workshop was probably the earliest, and examples of this school of carving frequently have a three-lobed leaf motif as a recurring feature of their decoration. In some cases the motif may be used in back-to-back pairs with intertwining tendrils, in others used in groups within flowing roundels. Such decoration, incorporated with a sword, a galley or panels of interlace, may be found on slabs at Iona, Inchkenneth, Oronsay and on Islay. Several well-preserved full-length effigies produced by the Iona school offer the most detailed picture of the warrior and the churchman of the 14th to 15th centuries; at Iona the effigy of Bricius MacKinnon is the most remarkable of this type, and that at Killean, in Kintyre, also illustrates the major features of contemporary armament. The details of the vestments of abbots and

93

Keil Church, Lochaline, Lochaber: north face of cross.

priests can also be seen on several slabs. The crosses in the Iona style, Campbeltown (no. 36), Inveraray (no.16), Kilchoman, Islay (NR 216632) and Lochaline (NM 670451) show many of the features of crisp tri-lobate foliaceous ornament that is the hall-mark of the school. A fragment of another type of cross may be seen at Borline on Skye (no. 35). Geological examination of the slabs has shown that many of them are of a stone not found on Iona; the unworked slabs of what is called a calc-chlorite-albite-schist were probably brought by sea from the Loch Sween area of Mid Argyll for carving on Iona.

The decoration of the Kintyre school of carving also uses foliaceous motifs, but frequently the three leaves or lobes are of similar size and in general the pattern flows less rhythmically than on stones of the Iona school; there is a tendency to clutter. Other major components of the decoration include swords, frequently with decorated pommels, and animals. Like the galleys of the Iona school and in contrast to those found on Oronsay, galleys on slabs of the Loch Awe school have their sails furled, eg Kilmory in Knapdale, and Killean in Kintyre (no. 46). The workshops of this tradition of carving may well have been associated with the abbey of Saddell in Kintyre; the abbey is now very ruined, but there is a collection of interesting stones including examples of Kintyre and Loch Awe types (NR 784320).

A looser tradition of carving based on Mid Argyll, Lorn and Loch Fyneside has been termed the Loch Awe school and described as 'artistically the least gifted of the West Highland schools of carving'. There is a greater use of locally available stone, perhaps, it is suggested, with the carvers travelling from area to area creating graveslabs to order. The decorative motifs are less assured, with haphazard leafy patterns visible at Kilmartin for example or illustrated here at Dalmally. Panels with a warrior, as at Dalmally, or with a long central sword, as at Kilmartin, are among the most frequent. At Kilmartin there are two of the rare warrior

effigies of this tradition of carving; a third carving in the collection here belongs to the Iona tradition.

A number of stones at Keills and Kilmory, Loch Sween in Knapdale, have features of decoration that draw them apart from the schools of carving already mentioned, some perhaps using motifs from more than one tradition. Because of their proximity to the likely source of stone for many of the slabs such cross-currents of style are not surprising. Nevertheless, the resultant carvings of the tentative Loch Sween school, including the cross of Alexander MacMillan at Kilmory, are some of the most original of the West Highland series. In the first half of the 16th century Oronsay Priory became an important focus for carving; the slabs have well-proportioned trilobe leafy patterns, claymores, naturalistic animals and galleys in full sail. Several of the effigies are in lower relief than those of the Iona school; one of the finest is the fragment of the graveslab of Prioress Anna (died 1543) on Iona itself, while others illustrate contemporary armament in fuller relief.

The styles of carving outlined here have a distribution that corresponds closely to the medieval dioceses of the Isles and Argyll, but more importantly to the geographical extent of the authority of the Lords of the Isles, patrons of the abbey of Iona. The main flowering of this style of carving occurs in the century or so before the final forfeiture of the Lordship in 1493 and the removal of this source of patronage from both Iona and Saddell. Oronsay Priory, however, was able to support a group of sculptors working primarily for the local market; a few late stones can be seen elsewhere including Iona, Islay and Lochaline.

It is not possible within the compass of our volume to list the free-standing crosses either of Early Christian or of late medieval date, nor all the lapidaria where important collections of stones are displayed. We have chosen representative stones from some of the major collections such as Iona and Oronsay, or highlighted

Kilchoman, Islay: east face of cross.

interesting stones from other ecclesiastical sites such as Killean (no. 46) or Dalmally (no. 38). Other important collections are at Saddell (NR 784320), Clachan of Glendaruel in Cowal (NR 994841; HBM), Kilberry (NR 709642; HBM), and Kilmartin (NR 834988; HBM). The medieval chapels of Keills (NR 691805) and Kilmory Knap (NR 702751) have been roofed by Scottish Development Department and now house well-displayed collections of stones, notably illustrating the work of the Loch Sween school.

Post-Reformation Churches

From an architectural point of view, perhaps the most important feature of reformed liturgical practice was the need for greater visibility and ready participation between the celebrant and the congregation. Initially medieval churches and chapels were rearranged internally to meet the new demands, with the communion table frequently occupying a focal point. In Argyll and the Isles there are, however, no examples of 17th century church building on any scale, a measure perhaps both of political and economic pressures as well as religious uncertainty of the area. In the 18th and early 19th centuries, however, with the planning of new towns at Inveraray and Bowmore, and the growing importance of older towns such as Campbeltown, new churches were built in contemporary styles (nos 14-16). Rural parishes too were provided with new churches more appropriate in plan to reformed worship. A' Chleit, in Kintyre (NR 681417), for example, replaced the medieval parish church of Killean (no. 46) in 1787. The new parish church at Dalmally (no. 38) built to an octagonal plan at the expense of the Earl of Breadalbane was opened in 1811. A comparable church in Gothic revival style is Kilmorlich Kirk, Cairndow, Cowal (1816) (NN 180107); 'gothic' ideals coupled with harling and pinnacles at the angles of the square tower offer a pleasing exterior. Snizort parish church, Kensaleyre, Skye (NG 421517) was originally

Pennygowan Chapel, Mull: cross-shaft.

Riasg Buidhe Cross, Colonsay.

designed by James Gillespie Graham in 1800, with several later additions; it was extensively renovated in 1979-80.

By Acts of Parliament in 1823 and 1824 many new churches and manses were built for communities in the Highlands and Islands; such 'Parliamentary Churches' were built to designs of Thomas Telford and a number of other architects including James Smith of Inverness. There were several standard ground-plans for churches and manses alike, with in some cases only the church being built and at others

only the manse. Twenty-one parishes in our area were thus provided, the majority with both church and manse. Among those that still survive, attention may be drawn to Duror (1827) (NM 993552) and Iona (1828) (NM 284242), and, in the Outer Isles, Berneray (1829) (NF 930820) and Staffin on Skye (1829) (NG 489673).

More recent churches of note, included in earlier sections of this guide, are St Conan's Church, Lochawe (no. 2), the Cathedral of St Columba and Christ's Church, Dunollie, both in Oban (no. 17).

Borline, Skye: fragment of cross-shaft (no. 35).

Campbeltown Cross, Campbeltown, Kintyre: north-east face (no. 36).

35 Churches and cross-shaft, Borline, Skye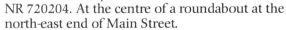

Medieval period.

NG 375259. Leave the B 8009 at Carbost, taking the road to Talisker and Glen Eynort. Where the road divides, follow the Glen Eynort road on the left to the end; walk along the shore to the walled graveyard.

In a pleasant wooded burial-ground stand the remains of two churches. The smaller, and probably older church, dedicated to St Maolrubha, has neat freestone surrounds to the doorway and three low windows; the early 18th century MacLeod memorials were probably placed there after the larger church had been built.

Outside the west end of the larger building are several fine carved slabs, and also part of a cross-shaft, carved in the Iona school, showing on one side the lower part of a crucifixion, with an abbot or bishop below, and on the other side a foliaceous pattern twined around a lion.

In this graveyard a fine carved font, now in NMAS, was found in the 19th century; the font is carved from a similar stone to that used at Rodel, Harris (no. 49), and has features that relate it to the West Highland traditions of carving, although in shape it conforms to English late medieval types.

36 Campbeltown Cross, Campbeltown, Kintyre

Later 14th century AD.

NR 720204. At the centre of a roundabout at the north-east end of Main Street.

The magnificent disc-headed cross now stands at the centre of a busy roundabout at the NE end of Main Street at the head of the Old Quay; this is not its original position, however, for it was probably brought from Kilkivan (NR 651201) in the early 17th century,

The front of the cross would have had a central figure of the crucifixion, now erased, with two unidentified saints to the top of the cross arm and St Mary and St John below. A vivid representation of St Michael slaying the dragon fills the left arm of the cross. Below the head of the cross is an empty panel and below that there was formerly a figure of a cleric with a chalice and a book, which alone now survive. The inscription which helps to date the cross to the latter part of the 14th century reads: 'This is the cross of Sir Yvarns MacEachern, sometime parson of Kylkecan, and Sir Andreas his son, parson of Kilchoman, who caused this cross to be made'. Beneath the inscription is a rather erratic panel of foliaceous decoration terminating in confronted beasts.

On the back of the cross the layout of the main panels of foliaceous or interlace decoration is highlighted by a series of paired figures: at the top there is a mermaid and sea monster, at the arms there are pairs of animals, and finally, at the base of the cross there are two pairs of confronted animals, now rather worn.

Campbeltown Cross, Campbeltown, Kintyre: detail of south-west face (no. 36).

and until the Second World War stood in front of the Town House, further up Main Street. The cross is carved out of the distinctive schist which comes from the area of Loch Sween; the decorative motifs are well thought out and arranged on both faces, with elaborate leaf scroll decoration on either side. Unfortunately several figures have been removed from the front of the cross creating three areas now void of decoration.

---

37 Teampull na Trionaid, Carinish, North Uist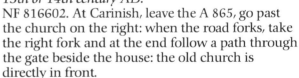
13th or 14th century AD.
NF 816602. At Carinish, leave the A 865, go past the church on the right: when the road forks, take the right fork and at the end follow a path through the gate beside the house: the old church is directly in front.

Teampull na Trionaid is one of the largest pre-Reformation churches in the Western Isles. It is reputed to have been built by Amie MacRurie, first wife of John, Lord of the Isles, and would thus date from the 14th century, though it may on architectural grounds belong to the preceding century. Measuring about 18.5 m by 6.5 m, the church is now ruinous; most of the south and east walls have fallen, but the north and west walls still stand to a considerable height and give some impression of the size of the building. It was described in the 19th century as having had freestone mouldings around both doors and windows, and carved figures set in the walls, but these had been removed, and the stone used for other purposes. At the west end the walls have a number of square holes in them, possibly used for scaffolding during building, or perhaps to support a gallery.

This building is connected with a smaller one to the north by a barrel-vaulted passage, which appears to be almost complete, though it is blocked with rubble, which may have contributed to its preservation. The smaller building, measuring about 8.5 m by 4 m and known as Teampull Clann a' Bhiocair or MacVicar's chapel, is in better condition, having both gables and the south wall nearly complete. Each wall has a

window, neatly built of local stone, and there are aumbries in both end walls.

Teampull na Trionaid is said to have been used as a refuge in 1601 by MacDonalds of North Uist who gathered their stock there for protection against a raiding party of MacLeods of Skye. The MacLeods were routed at the battle of Carinish not far from the church.

---

38 Parish Church, Dalmally, Lorn
Early 19th century AD.
NN 167275. Situated to the north of the Dalmally Hotel.

The unusual octagonal church at Dalmally, serving the parish of Glenorchy and Inishail, was designed for the 4th Earl of Breadalbane in 1808 by an Edinburgh architect, James Elliot, who was at that time working on the Earl's castle at Taymouth, in Perthshire. The church, probably the third to occupy the island site since the medieval period, was opened for worship in 1811. The interior, which was re-arranged in 1898, has two side banks and one central bank of pews facing the pulpit at the west end; additional seating being provided in a horse-shoe shaped gallery. The ceiling is flat, but the illustration shows the complex system of internal timbers that holds this unsupported span in position.

The churchyard contains a range of late-medieval stones of some importance, including an example of the Loch Awe School of carving, with border, plant scroll with animals and figure of the warrior at the top typical of that school. The second stone, much smaller than is usual and presumably the graveslab of a child, is also of the Loch Awe School. The third stone, later perhaps in the West Highland sequence of carving, is also of interest because it has been appropriated at a later date as the inscription shows, '1819 James McNicoll, Achallader'.

Parish Church, Dalmally, Lorn (no. 38).

99

Parish Church, Dalmally, Lorn: interior (no. 38).

Parish Church, Dalmally, Lorn: detail of roof structure (no. 38).

Parish Church, Dalmally, Lorn: graveslab of child (no. 38).

Parish Church, Dalmally, Lorn: graveslab (no. 38).

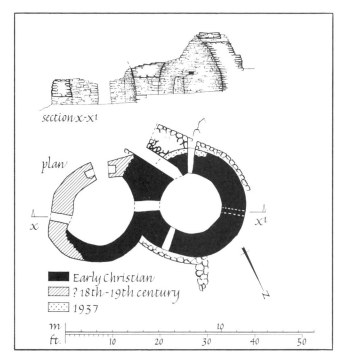

section x-x¹

plan

x ——— x¹

N

■ Early Christian
▨ ?18th-19th century
▨ 1957

m
ft.
10 10 20 30 40 50

Eileach an Naoimh, Garvellachs: beehive cells from south-east (no. 39).

39 Eileach an Naoimh, Early Christian Monastery, Garvellachs

Early Christian and medieval periods.
NM 640097. By hired boat from Toberonochy, Luing; subject to weather conditions.
HBM (SDD).

The journey to the Garvellachs can be an adventure in itself and it is important to choose settled weather. Such a remote island was the ideal choice for a small community of the early church dedicated to a contemplative life. The remains of this period comprise an unusual double-beehive cell, a grave-enclosure, and a series of larger enclosures or burial grounds. There is also a church of medieval date. The double beehive cell uses the sandstone slabs of the island to full advantage to form two round chambers within walls which are about 1.5 m thick. The slabs of the inner wall faces have been laid in overlapping courses to form a corbelled interior. Each chamber has a doorway from the outside and there is also a passage to provide access between the chambers. The structure has been partly restored in 1937, and it is now difficult to be certain of the original arrangements in some places; the use of mortar appears to date from the reconstruction and would certainly not have been part of the original building-method.

Situated on an elevated position 200 m to the south west, there is a circular kerbed enclosure measuring about 3 m in diameter with two upright slabs within the line of the kerb, one of which bears an incised cross. This kerbed setting has been traditionally identified as the burial place of Eithne, St Columba's mother.

Other features of early date include a small underground cell, a chapel and a burial-ground, in which there is a cross-marked slab of the type usually described as a grave-marker. Two further crosses are now in RMS.

101

40 Eye Church, Lewis
Medieval period.
NB 484322. Signposted on the A 866 at the east end of the sea defences: follow a track to the north for a short distance.

St Columba's church at Eye, the burying place of the MacLeods of Lewis, is believed to have been built on the site of the cell of St Catan, a contemporary of St Columba. The present buildings are probably medieval and clearly there are two periods of construction.

Glendale, Skye: graveslab showing a musician with a harp (no. 41).

The eastern building is probably the older and is one of the largest pre-Reformation churches in the Western Isles. There are indications that the walls have been raised by over a metre and alterations made in the south wall; the original entrance near the middle of this wall is now blocked and the doorway is a later opening with a timber lintel. The only windows are on the south side and high in the east gable. The west end is pierced by a round-headed doorway leading to the smaller building. Local red sandstone is incorporated in its doors and windows. There is a blocked entrance on the south side of this building, and there have been windows in both side walls and the west wall; below the window, in the west gable, is an arched recess which may once have held a tomb.

Two carved stones are now clamped to the walls of the larger building. One depicts a warrior in a quilted coat, wearing a pointed helmet and grasping a spear and sword. The carving is probably 15th century and is popularly supposed to represent Roderick, 7th chief of the MacLeods of Lewis. The stone opposite, carved with a complex group of animals and foliage, has a Latin inscription which, in translation reads: 'Here lies Margareta, daughter of Rodericus MacLeod of Lewis, widow of Lachlan MacKinnon. She died in 1503'.

41 Carved Slab, Glendale, Skye
Medieval period.
NG 175497. At Glendale, in a walled burial-ground a short distance north of the B 884.

This stone shows the figure of a man playing a harp, a rare feature on a stone of this type; below is a sword, with a foliaceous design on one side, and on the other a mitred figure, a chalice, and two badly worn panels; one possibly representing a casket.

Inchkenneth Chapel, Mull: graveslabs (no. 42)

42 Inchkenneth Chapel, Mull

13th to 15th century.
NM 437354. On the island of Inchkenneth close to the jetty.
HBM (SDD).

Although now roofless, the chapel on Inchkenneth offers the visitor a good impression of the scale of the parish church of the mid-13th century; the dedication to St Cainnech of Aghaboe, a contemporary of St Columba, however, implies an earlier foundation of which there is now no trace. The chancel and nave form a single unit, with the floor of the chancel set a little lower than that of the nave. There was little embellishment either round the doorway on the north side or the windows, one each on the north and south wall of the chancel, and a pair of lancet windows on the east. Twin-light east windows are a characteristic feature of the comparatively simple churches of this period in the west. Dr Johnson, who visited Inchkenneth in 1772, noted 'On one side of the altar is a bas relief of the blessed Virgin, and by it lies a little bell; which, though cracked, and without a clapper, has remained there for ages, guarded only by the venerableness of the place. The ground round the chapel is covered with grave-stones of Chiefs and ladies . . .'

The graveslabs form an important collection and several are now protected within the chapel; two are illustrated here: one with a sword above a galley without a sail, with plant-scroll decoration on either side of the sword; the second has heavier more formalised plant decoration with paired animal ornament near the head and a hound and stag at the foot. The second stone is a good example of the Iona School of carving of about the 14th to 15th century AD.

Inchkenneth Chapel, Mull: general view from south-west (no. 42).

103

43 Iona

There is a regular ferry service for pedestrians from Fionnphort at the western tip of the Ross of Mull. All the sites are well signposted and access is comparatively easy. The island is largely owned by the National Trust for Scotland, with the exception of the Abbey and associated buildings which are owned by the Iona Cathedral Trust.

The small island of Iona has played an important, if intermittent, role in the religious, and indeed political, life of what is now Scotland for over fourteen hundred years; today's visitors frequently share a sense of devotion to the past and present traditions that Iona contributes to the religious life of Scotland and beyond, as well as a sense of wonder at the preservation of the great crosses, over a thousand years old, and at the magnificence of the restored abbey against the rugged back-drop of Mull. A helpful guidebook *Iona,* by J G Dunbar and I Fisher, will take the visitor on a more detailed tour than is possible here, and this section is intended mainly to set some of the more important features into the broader context of our own volume.

The long journey across Mull to Iona gives the modern visitor a feeling of remoteness that it did not possess for the seaborne traveller of the mid first millennium AD; in 563 St Columba landed on this little island with twelve companions to found a community of religious contemplation. The impact of the saint's preaching and his journeyings and those of his followers through Pictland and among the Scots had a profound effect on the political complexion of Scotland. Today the spirit of Columba is evoked in the restored Benedictine abbey founded around 1200, but there are still slight remains of the Early Christian monastery. The early monastery would have been surrounded by a rampart and ditch enclosing the timber church, the cells of the monks, and the communal buildings such as the *scriptorium,* where books were kept and copied; a corner of this massive earthwork survives to the north-west of the abbey (NM 286247), and there is a further stretch to the west, but most has now been ploughed flat.

The high crosses provide the most striking evidence of the religious fervour and artistic achievement of the community from the middle of the 8th century to the early 9th century. The fragments of St Oran's Cross, the earliest of the group, are now in the Nunnery Museum, but the other three stand near the west end of the nave of the abbey; St John's Cross is also in a fragmentary state, but a reproduction stands on its site, and, following consolidation, the cross itself will be displayed again on Iona. The ringed-cross was not carved in one piece, but was formed of at least eight components pieced together by means of mortice and tenon joints. The decoration comprises well thought out panels of interlace and of motifs based on serpents-and-bosses, a pattern also found on several

Pictish stones. A date in the mid to late 8th century is currently suggested for St John's Cross.

The best-known and most complete cross, that of St Martin, has panels in a similar serpent-and-boss design on its east face and a series of figural scenes on the west face including the Virgin and Child at the centre. David with musicians and Abraham's sacrifice of Isaac were carved at the centre of the shaft. A date in the second half of the 8th century is usually suggested for the cross. The fragment of St Matthew's Cross shows part of the Temptation of Adam and Eve, but even the surviving decoration is very worn. The various artistic parallels that can be drawn for the decoration or carved detail show that the Iona carvers, and by implication the religious life of the community as a whole, were benefiting from and contributing to the interaction of several artistic traditions from Ireland, Pictland and Northumbria. Sometime after 800, however, as a result of pressure from Viking raiders, the greater part of the religious community was transferred to Kells in Ireland, and for the next four hundred years there was only a token religious presence on the island.

The earliest of the three major ecclesiastical buildings on the island is St Oran's Chapel (NM 285244), the most striking feature of which is the round arch of the west doorway; the middle row of decorative stonework was ornamented with heads, but these are now very worn. The main feature of the interior is a tomb recess of the later 15th century.

The abbey (NM 286245) is the most dramatic ecclesiastical building in the west of Scotland; the sequence of building is outlined in the guidebook already mentioned, illustrating the fortunes of the abbey from its foundation around 1200 to 1500. The nave has been much restored, but the choir, transepts and south aisle contain many exquisite medieval carved details. The cloister has been one of the most successful features of recent restoration, with the twin-

St Oran's Chapel, Iona (no. 43).

side of the cloister are of early 13th century date, but the present cloister and the refectory on the south-west side date to about 1500.

There are two important collections of Early Christian and medieval stones on Iona: one in St Ronan's Church, adjacent to the Nunnery, and the other in the Abbey Museum where there is an extensive collection of Early Christian grave-markers and medieval grave-slabs. Beside the road between the Nunnery and the Abbey, MacLean's Cross is a fine late-medieval sculpture of late 15th century date; on the front there is a representation of the crucifixion with elaborate plant ornament on the shaft; the back of the shaft has similar ornament with two animals at the top and a mounted warrior at its base   HBM (SDD).

The parish church and manse (NM 284242) belong to the group of 'parliamentary churches' mentioned earlier; the church is of rectangular plan (one of the standard designs) and was completed in 1828.

Quite apart from the architectural treasures on Iona, the island itself offers many beautiful views; the visitor to the Bay at the Back of the Ocean enjoys the natural peace of the island in the same spirit as that of St Columba's followers. Dun Cul Bhuirg, the only iron-age monument on Iona, is not well preserved, but several sections of the wall are still visible, and it offers wide views of the western side of the island (NM 264246); access, however, is difficult.

At Port an Fhir-bhreige (NM 262219) there are over fifty small cairns as well as two large mounds all made of beach pebbles and there is a tradition that they were made by monks and pilgrims as acts of penitence. Just a little to the east is the bay known as Port na Curaich, or St Columba's Bay, where the saint is supposed first to have set foot on Iona; the mound traditionally associated with Columba's boat (curragh) is, however, natural.

pillars of the cloister arcades supporting paired capitals, with leaf or stem ornament, from which spring the main arches. Perhaps in the cloister the contemplative calm of the medieval abbey is best recreated.

The nunnery (NM 284240) was founded about 1200 and belonged to the Augustinian order; the church and chapter-house on the north-east and south-east

*St Martin's Cross, Iona: west face
(no. 43).*

*St Mary's Abbey, Iona: west front of
Abbey Church and crosses (no. 43).*

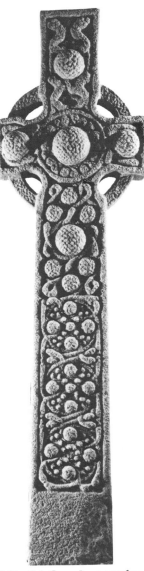

*St Martin's Cross, Iona: east face
(no. 43).*

*Port an Fhir-bhreige, Iona: cairns
(no. 43).*

44 Kilbarr Church and chapels, Barra ♿²

Medieval and later periods.
NF 705073. Take the road north to Eoligarry from
the A 888; the chapels are immediately beside the
road in the burial ground at Eoligarry.

On the eastern slope of Ben Eoligarry are the remains
of a medieval church dedicated to St Barr (Cille
Bharra) and two chapels, a group similar to that at
Howmore, South Uist (NF 758364). Only parts of the
side walls of the church still stand; the doorway is on
the north side and three windows survive, two at the
east end providing light for the altar. On the inside the
windows have a pointed arch formed by two lintels set
diagonally, while on the outside there is a round-
headed arch.

One chapel is largely ruinous, and the west gable
stands only to a height of about 2 m. The other is well
preserved and has recently been re-roofed to provide a
shelter for several carved slabs which were in the
cemetery. This chapel, or perhaps burial-aisle, is
probably later in date than the two other buildings; the
entrance was in the west gable, but there is a
secondary entrance in the south wall, and there are
narrow slit windows in the side walls and east gable.

There are several slabs of interest, including the only
West Highland graveslabs on Barra: two of these are
decorated with a claymore and foliaceous designs;
another is badly weathered, but a galley and a deer can
still be seen. An unusual stone found in 1865 is now in
NMAS; on the front there is an interlace-filled cross
with side panels of scrolls and key pattern. The back
has a runic inscription, which reads 'after Thorgerth,
Steinar's daughter, this cross was raised' and dates to
the 10th or early 11th century.

45 Old Parish Church, Kildalton, and Kildalton ♿² Cross, Islay

Early Christian and medieval periods.
NR 458508. Situated 11 km NE of Port Ellen;
signposted.
HBM (SDD): Cross.

The simple church dating to the late 12th or early
13th century is an oblong building, now heavily
restored, although some interior features including the
remains of a piscina and an aumbry may still be seen.
What is remarkable about Kildalton is the presence of
one of the most complete Early Christian crosses still
to be found in Scotland, dating to the second half of
the eighth century. The decoration is clearly
comparable to the crosses on Iona and demonstrates
that this part of the Dalriadan possessions was within
a similar artistic ambit. The ringed cross has been
carved from a single slab of epidiorite. At the top of the
shaft on the east face there is a representation of the
Virgin and Child flanked by angels; on the arms of the
cross the scenes have most recently been identified as
Cain's murder of Abel, and Abraham's sacrifice of
Isaac, while at the centre of the upper shaft of the cross
it is possible that, surmounted by a pair of angels, the
carvers have shown David slaying the lion. The
remaining more decorative panels on this side
demonstrate the carvers' expertise in serpent-and-boss
ornament and in curvilinear interlace. On the west
side serpent-and-boss patterns run in restrained riot
creating a three-dimensional decoration, with four
lions around the central boss.

There are at least seventeen West Highland graveslabs
both inside the church and in the surrounding
graveyard which underline the importance of
Kildalton from Early Christian times to the medieval
period, when the present parish church was built. The
slabs are of diverse manufacture and belong to four of
the five schools of carving outlined by Steer and
Bannerman, Iona, Loch Awe, Loch Sween and
Oronsay.

Kildalton Cross, Islay.
(no. 45).

109

46 Old Parish Church, Killean, Kintyre
Medieval period.
NR 695445. At Killean on the west side of the road between Tarbert and Campbeltown.

The former parish church of Killean is of interest both as a surviving fragment of twelfth century architecture and as the focus for a wide variety of funerary monuments. The church is now ruined, but three periods of construction can be seen: the nave (12th century), the chancel with the remains of an elaborately decorated east window (early 13th century), and the north aisle, which was taken over in the last century as the burial aisle of the MacDonalds of Largie, is originally of fifteenth century work.

An Early Christian cross from the site is now in Campbeltown Museum; there are several medieval tombstones set in the north aisle of the church, and several interesting later stones in the churchyard. Three of the medieval stones are illustrated here: the first has a fine sword to one side of the slab with two stems on the other; the inscription which is in Lombardic capitals reads 'John, Son of Ewan, had this stone made for himself and for his father'. The animal ornament below the inscription contains an unusual collection of beasts: a salmon is being chased by an otter, followed by a stag pursued by hounds. The stone belongs to the Kintyre School and dates to the 15th century. The second stone, of similar date, is a good example of balanced foliaceous patterning round a sheathed sword. The third slab is a beautifully carved example of a fully-armed knight: he has a pointed bascinet (helmet), protective mail covers his shoulders and neck and he wears a long sword with belt fastenings and a ribbed tunic. The stone belongs to the Iona School and is of 14th–15th century date.

Several 19th century headstones in Kintyre cemeteries provide vivid insights into contemporary agricultural life; here at Killean the stone commemorating Donald McKinnon, who died in 1810, illustrates ploughing with a two-horse team.

Old Parish Church, Killean, Kintyre: general view from south-east (no. 46).

Old Parish Church, Killean, Kintyre: graveslab showing plough-team (no. 46).

Old Parish Church, Killean,
Kintyre: graveslabs (no. 46)

47 Cathedral of St Moluag and Parish Church, Lismore

Medieval and later periods.
NM 860434. On the main island road running from the Port Appin Ferry to Achnacroish and 4 km from the latter.

Although now much altered, the parish church of Lismore occupies the choir of the 14th century cathedral of the medieval diocese of Argyll dedicated to St Moluag and is thus one of the earliest churches still used for worship. The cathedral nave to the west barely survives and the tower which was at the west end of the nave is visible only at foundation level. The medieval church was, however, roofless by 1679, and its present state is a result of rebuilding in 1749 at which time the walls were lowered by as much as 3 m before it was re-roofed. The external buttresses on the south side are original features, but the round-headed windows appear to date to the 18th century restoration. The interior offers at first sight only the impression of a presbyterian church at the turn of the century, but on the south wall the piscina, sedilia(the seating for the more important clergy) as well as an original doorway still remain visible. The northern doorway is more elaborate with the arch moulding springing from the carved heads of a bishop and a cleric.

Several interesting medieval graveslabs are preserved in the church, and others are in the graveyard.

St Moluag was an Irish saint who founded a Christian community on Lismore traditionally between 561 and 564, and from here he travelled extensively in Pictland; to him are attributed the foundations, among others, of churches at Rosemarkie, in Ross and Cromarty, and Mortlach, in Banffshire. Thus the present church bears testimony not only to the activities of one of the earliest missionaries to what is now Scotland and to the creation of the diocese of Argyll with its see on Lismore in the late 12th century, but also to the later rebuilding and to the subsequent sensitive restoration of the medieval features by Ian Lindsay in 1956.

Cathedral of St Moluag and Parish Church, Lismore: general view from south-east (no. 47).

Iona: village and abbey (no. 43).

Dun Aisgain, Mull (no. 55).

Glebe Cairn, Kilmartin,
Mid Argyll, (no. 71).

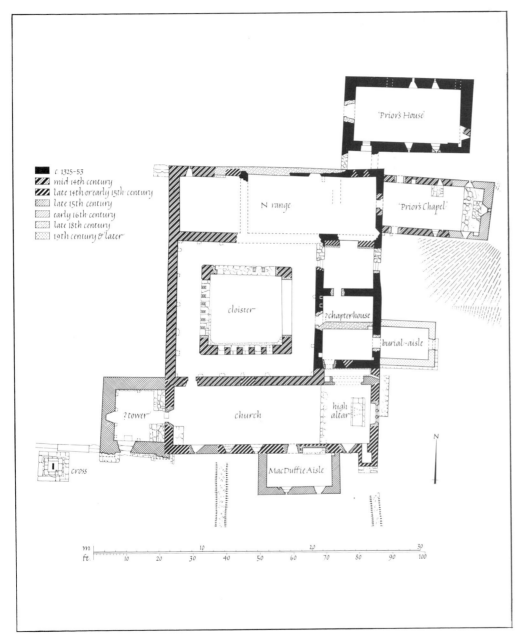

c 1325–53

mid 14th century

late 14th or early 15th century

late 15th century

early 16th century

late 18th century

19th century & later

'Prior's House'

'Prior's Chapel'

N range

cloister

?chapter-house

burial-aisle

high altar

?tower

church

cross

MacDuffie Aisle

N

m | | | | | 10 | | | | 20 | | | | 30
ft. | 10 | 20 | 30 | 40 | 50 | 60 | 70 | 80 | 90 | 100

48 Oronsay Priory, Oronsay

Medieval and later periods.

NR 349889. Oronsay is a tidal island and access on foot or by post-bus is regulated by the time of low tide; it is important to check locally.

Oronsay Priory, a house of Augustinian canons, was founded in the second quarter of the 14th century by John, Lord of the Isles and is one of the rare medieval foundations in Argyll that lacks any Early Christian antecedent, though there was certainly earlier activity on Colonsay at, for example, Riasg Buidhe (p. 158). The priory is of interest from an architectural point of view and there is also an extensive series of graveslabs displayed in the building known as the 'Prior's House'. There are also important late medieval crosses, particularly that known as the Oronsay Cross situated outside the west end of the priory church.

The ruins of the priory form a compact group of buildings set to the north of the church: the church is aligned east and west with the altar at the east end and the side chapel known as the MacDuffie Chapel to the south; at the west end is the baptistry, possibly the basal part of an intended tower. To the north of the church is the small cloister with a further chapel and the chapter house at the east side. The refectory and presumably the dormitory were on the north side of the cloister, with the building known as the Prior's Chapel projecting from the east end. A detached building a little to the north is known as the Prior's House. Although some of the buildings may be as early as the mid-14th century foundation, most of the surviving remains belong to a succession of building phases between the late 14th and early 16th centuries, not all now easy to disentangle. One of the most dramatic features of the church is the large window at the east end with thin mullions dividing it into three arched lights; this is of late 15th century date. The cloister is also of interest, although parts have been largely reconstructed. The south side of the cloister

Oronsay Cross, Oronsay: west face (no. 48).

Oronsay Cross, Oronsay: east face (no. 48).

arcade has round-headed arches which appear to be part of the original design; the unusual gable arches of the west side were re-modelled in the early 16th century and reconstructed in 1883. Two inscribed slabs are of particular interest as they record in Latin 'Canon Celestinus, director of this work' and 'Mael-Sechlainn O Cuinn, mason, made this work'.

The Oronsay Cross is one of the masterpieces of planning and execution of interlaced foliage design. On the front there is a figure of Christ crucified at the centre of the cross surrounded by ribbons of interlace; leafy roundels take up much of the shaft, but there are two little animals and a worn Latin inscription: 'This is the cross of Colinus, son of Cristinus MacDuffie'. On the back foliate roundels again occupy the shaft with one arched to accommodate two little animals. On the socket stone there is an incised circle with rays which appears to be a worn 'mass-clock'. A further Latin inscription reads in translation 'Mael-Sechlainn O Cuinn, mason, made this cross'. O Cuinn was probably trained in Iona and the cross is certainly of the Iona School, and he was probably also the mason responsible for the reconstruction of the priory cloister in the early 16th century. This cross is one of the last major achievements of the Iona School.

To the east of the 'Prior's Chapel', a cross-head has been amalgamated with a cross-shaft to which it was not originally joined; the figure in the head of the cross, which has been carved with considerable skill and attention to detail, has been identified as St John the Evangelist.

Over thirty graveslabs have been brought together in the 'Prior's House'; as there is no artificial light, visitors may find a torch useful to examine detail. Four representative stones are described and illustrated here. A characteristic graveslab of the Iona School has a central sword with the hand-grip attachments terminating in a round pommel. The plant decoration on either side of the blade is surmounted by a small

animal. The rectangular feature at the bottom of the sword is a chest with a small carrying-handle like that now used on a cash-box. A superb effigy of the Iona School retains much of the crisp detail with which the armour was carved: the bascinet (helmet), mail shoulder-piece and an aketon (quilted coat); the stitched portions, which would have been filled with protective padding are clearly indicated. The sword and the fittings of the sword belt are shown. The figures at the feet are perhaps symbolically unbuckling the spurs. Such an effigy is of 14th to 15th century date. The decoration of this slab shares features with the Loch Sween School, particularly in the layout of the animals and the interlace ornament; it has been suggested that the carver of this slab may also have

been responsible for the fine cross of Alexander MacMillan at Kilmory. The stone that commemorates Murchardus MacDuffie is one of the liveliest examples of the Oronsay School with crisp detail both in the animal ornament and the galley at the base of the slab. The inscription reads 'Here lies Murchardus MacDuffie of Colonsay who died in the year of Our Lord 1539; and Mariota MacLean caused me to be made'. At the top of the slab there is a stag with two does behind him, beleaguered by a pack of hounds. The sword shows details of the hilt with decorated handle and traces of the chape with well thought out leaf pattern on either side. The galley is in full sail, one of the hallmarks of the Oronsay School, and details of the rigging and the rudder are still clearly visible.

Oronsay Priory, Oronsay: graveslabs (no. 48).

Oronsay Priory, Oronsay: effigy (no. 48).

49 St Clement's Church, Rodel, Harris

Medieval period.
NG 047831. At Rodel, at the southern end of
A 859.
HBM (SDD).

St Clement's Church is the most impressive of the pre-Reformation churches remaining in the Western Isles. It has been restored on several occasions, the last being in 1873, but most of the walls and the greater part of the tower are medieval in date. Rodel is the burial place of many of the MacLeods of Dunvegan and Harris.

The church is built on uneven ground; the nave and choir are continuous, and there are two transepts not precisely opposite each other and roofed at a lower level than the main structure. The tower at the west end is built on rock at a higher level than the church and has a ground-floor entrance on the west side and an intramural stair leading up to this level from the church. Most of the windows are square-headed but the east window has a pointed arch with three trefoil-headed lights and above these there is a wheel window with six spokes.

The south wall of the church has two magnificent tombs built into it; one was built in 1528 for Alexander MacLeod (also known as Alasdair Crotach of Dunvegan), although he did not in fact die for about another twenty years. This outstanding monument has a figure of a man in plate armour lying in a

St Clement's Church, Rodel, Harris (no. 49).

recessed arch. The back of the arch is decorated with panels carved with a variety of scenes: at the top are angels on either side of a radiant sun; the middle of the next row is occupied by the Virgin and Child with a bishop on one side and St Clement on the other; at the ends of the row are a castle (see p. 72) and a galley under sail. The bottom row shows a hunting scene of men holding dogs and a knight with a sword. They are observing a group of deer which features in the next panel. Beyond are St Michael and Satan weighing souls, and the inscription explaining for whom the tomb was made 'This tomb was prepared by Lord Alexander, son of Willielmus MacLeod, Lord of Dunvegan, in the year of Our Lord 1528'. The front of the arch is decorated with further panels. At the top is

a representation of God the Father holding a crucifix between his knees, flanked by angels, and there are four panels on either side, three containing pairs of figures, representing the apostles, and one containing an angel holding a censer. The effigy of the knight is carved in dark hornblende schist, while the panels are of pale freestone, possibly from Mull; the panels on the front of the arch have plain pieces of schist between them and the whole group is edged with schist.

The other tomb also has an armoured man lying under an arch; there is a partly illegible inscription at the back of the recess: 'This is the tomb prepared by Lord . . . in the year of Our Lord 1539'. Above the

St Clement's Church, Rodel, Harris: the tomb of Alexander MacLeod of Dunvegan (no. 49).

rounded arch a pointed border encloses a crucifixion scene, with a figure on either side of the cross.

A third effigy is placed against the north wall, beside the door; the helmet, plate armour with mail and sword show that it is of 16th century date.

Several carved graveslabs are now set against one wall of the north transept. There is also, on the sill of a south window, an unusual small disc-headed cross, bearing on one side Christ crucified and on the other an interlace pattern. The contrast between the dark schist and the pale freestone of the MacLeod tomb is reflected in the arches of the transepts, and light and dark stone is also used alternately in the quoins of the tower.

The tower has a cabled string-course of schist about half way up, broken at the corners and centre of each wall face. Below it are plain slit windows, and above small lancets. At the top of the tower is a crenellated parapet.

Several carvings are set into the tower walls in spaces partially framed by the string course: on the west wall there is a figure that may be St Clement above two unidentified men; on the south wall there is a squatting female figure nursing a child; on the east wall a worn panel may represent a boat; and on the north wall there is a bull's head.

50* St Mary's Chapel, Rothesay, Bute

13th–14th century AD.
NS 086637. Situated 0.8 km south of Rothesay; check with the custodian at Rothesay Castle. HBM (SDD).

The ruins of this chapel stand next to the parish church of Rothesay; the chapel known as St Mary's or Lady Kirk may be as early as the 13th century in date, though later dates have also been proposed. It is now of interest primarily for the two well-preserved recessed canopy-tombs at the middle of each of the side-walls, and an effigy in the West Highland tradition. The effigy is that of a warrior with the arms of the Menteiths and it is likely that it is of mid-14th century date, indeed this may be one of the earliest surviving carved armorials in Scotland. The church is presumably on the site of an earlier foundation, for in 1816 the fragments of an unusual Early Christian cross slab, now in Bute Museum, were uncovered during clearing operations.

St Clement's Church, Rodel, Harris (no. 49), detail of Macleod tomb

St Mary's Chapel, Rothesay, Bute: tomb (no. 50).

51 St Blane's Church, St Blane's, Bute

Early Christian and later 12th century AD.
NS 094534. Near the southern tip of Bute,
signposted.
HBM (SDD).

Standing in one of the most beautiful settings of all the
medieval churches in western Scotland, St Blane's
Church is dedicated to a saint and missionary of the
Early Christian church, who was born in Bute in the
6th century. The medieval church reflects the siting of
an Early Christian foundation, possibly an offshoot
from some larger establishment, and several early
crosses have been found and are still visible here.
Excavations in 1896 also uncovered several pieces of
slate with interlace and animal designs, comparable to
those from Dunadd (no. 54), now in RMS. The crosses
apart, perhaps the main surviving feature is to the
north and east of the church where there is an arc of
the enclosure wall, now about 0.8 m high and 1.5 m
wide. An enigmatic circular stone-built foundation,
known as 'The Cauldron', is situated to the north-west
of the church at the base of the cliff. It measures about
10 m by 9.3 m within an unusually thick wall (2.5 m
overall) which is still almost 2 m in height; there is a
well-built entrance on the south-east side. This is
unlikely to be a defensive structure because of its
overlooked position, but it finds no ready parallel
among early monastic buildings. Other foundations to
the north and south have been interpreted as monastic
cells, but this is not certain.

The church comprised a nave and a small chancel,
with the elaborate decoration of the chancel arch in
true Romanesque style suggesting a date in the later
12th century. The chevron pattern which forms the
main element of the arch (with a small Greek Cross in
a circle at its apex) and the decoration of the capitals of
the supporting columns are particularly fine.

52 Clach Ard, Tote, Skye

6th-7th century AD.
NG 421491. Take the B 8036, between the
Portree-Uig and the Portree-Dunvegan roads; turn
north-west along the small road leading to Tote;
the stone is about 400 m along the road on the
right-hand side.

The stone is some 1.3 m in height and about 0.5 m
broad with a series of symbols on its southern face;
there is a crescent and V-rod at the top, a double disc
and Z-rod beneath and formerly there was a mirror
and comb symbol near the bottom, but this is no
longer visible. There is a local tradition that the stone
was incorporated into the shoemaker's house at Tote
till about 1880, perhaps as a door jamb.

*Clach Ard, Tote, Skye: Pictish
symbol stone (no. 52).*

St Mary's Abbey, Iona: cloister (no. 43).

121

7

PREHISTORIC MONUMENTS

The prehistoric monuments of the west of Scotland offer the student and visitor alike one of the most comprehensive arrays of sites of almost all periods. Because many were built in stone they remain in a remarkable state of preservation and, although we know of sites destroyed in the course of agricultural improvements or quarrying, as in all areas of Britain, a large number of exciting monuments remain. Patterns of settlement can be built up for many areas during the period from about 4000 BC based on the distribution of chambered tombs, cairns, iron-age fortifications and small finds of many periods. The sites we have chosen to describe in detail in the Gazetteer are chosen from many superb sites; these are laid out in reverse chronological order, as though you are exploring the monuments from the standpoint of today back in time: the fortifications of the iron age; then the earlier cairns, stone circles, standing stones and rock carvings of the bronze age and perhaps earlier times too; finally we offer some of the best preserved chambered cairns of the earliest agricultural communities of the west coast.

IRON-AGE FORTIFICATIONS

The major monuments of the second half of the 1st millennium BC and the first half of the 1st millennium AD are stone-walled fortifications. Simple stone-walled forts are sometimes impressive more for their situation than for their surviving

Ardnacross, Mull, standing stones

remains. A feature of building construction at several different periods was the use of a timber framework within the stone wall in order to increase the stability; in some cases a wooden lacing was used only at the entrance. In the event of fire, however, either accidentally or as a result of enemy attack, the timberwork generated such extremes of heat that the stone core fused into vitrified lumps, often still visible today, as at Carradale (no. 53) and Dunagoil, Bute (NS 084531). Characteristic of the west of Scotland are small stone-walled forts, with thick well-built stone walls and internal timber buildings; the shape of such 'duns' was often determined by the rocky knoll on which they were sited for additional defence. Duns were in use over a long period from the later 1st millennium BC into historical times, although the majority were probably built in the first few centuries AD. Many sites in the Hebrides are on small partly 'improved' islands in lochs, with submerged causeways leading to them. Such naturally defensible structures continued in use into historical times, for example, Dun Ban, Loch Caravat, North Uist (NF 843608), a mortared square-cornered structure, and Caisteal Bheagram, South Uist (NF 761371). Duns were in effect well-defended homesteads, and were the focus for small farming communities. In addition to the duns listed here, many other well-preserved sites might be included in an itinerary; others, however, survive today merely as rings of rubble in which a few facing-stones may still be visible. On Mull, An Sean Dun is sited characteristically on an elongated ridge

123

Dun an t-Siamain, North Uist.

Dun an Sticir, North Uist.

Dun Mara, Lewis.

124

Mesolithic shell-mounds, Oronsay.

(NM 431562); in Mid Argyll, Druim an Duin
(NR 781913) is interesting as there are two doorways
with door-jambs, the better preserved also has a bar-
hole with an opposing socket, and a cell. In Kintyre,
Dun Skeig (NR 757571) has three periods of building:
a fort, with a superimposed timber-laced structure,
which was subsequently burnt and became vitrified,
and a later dun which incorporated pieces of vitrified
material. At the mouth of the Borgadel Water in
Kintyre (NR 625061), there is a well preserved, but less
accessible, dun.

The most innovative of iron-age fortifications—the
broch—has taxed Scottish archaeologists for
generations. Broch towers were skilfully built using a
distinctive type of wall-construction: an inner and an
outer skin of drystone masonry were bonded together
by a series of horizontal slabs spanning the hollow
space between them. Such a sophisticated design is
clearly the culmination of a period of experimentation.
A ledge or scarcement often runs round the inner face,
and this was probably designed to support timber
buildings. Excavations at Dun Mor, Vaul, Tiree
(no. 64) showed that the broch was built about the
middle of the 1st century AD. The structural
similarities are such that it is likely that the majority of
the 'classic' brochs in the west were built about the

same time. Brochs are not confined to the west of
Scotland, however, and some of the best preserved are
in the Northern Isles, Caithness and Sutherland; there
is also a group in southern Scotland; most of these
seem to lack a gallery at the lowest levels and they are
thus thought to be later on typological grounds. The
question of the origin of this style of architecture is
fraught with many difficulties: one possible area is
Orkney where there is a tradition of building round
stone houses with complex internal arrangements and
where recent excavation of broch-like structures has
produced radiocarbon dates in the 6th century BC;
another is Skye and the adjacent mainland where
there is also a convincing series of structures that may
be ancestral to brochs, including for example Dun
Ardtreck (no. 58), from the earliest levels of which
there was a radiocarbon date in the middle of the first
century BC.

Further examples of brochs not considered sufficiently
well preserved to be included in this volume, but
nevertheless of some interest to the enthusiast, may be
seen at Dun Borodale, Raasay, Skye (NG 554363), at
Fiskavaig, Skye (NG 318333) on a good defensive
hilltop site, at Dun Torcuill, North Uist (NF 888737)
on an islet on a loch and Dun Bragair, Lewis (NB
285474), again on an islet.

53 Carradale Point, Fort, Kintyre

Mid to late 1st millennium BC.

NR 815364. To the south of Carradale village, first by track then along the shoreline at low tide.

This fort occupies the highest part of a small tidal island, the southern extremity of which is Carradale Point, and access is only possible at low tide. The fort is about 56 m by 23 m within a thick wall, which was originally composed of stone and timber; several stretches of outer facing-stones remain on the west and south-east sides of the fort. Particularly remarkable, however, are the massive lumps of vitrified material, the remains of the stone core of the wall fused together as a result of a great conflagration. It is possible that there was a larger number of timbers on the east side of the fort, where the vitrifaction is heaviest, for it was the burning timbers that created the draughts which allowed the fierce heat necessary for the fusing together of the stones. At one time it was thought that this was a deliberate act on the part of the prehistoric builders, but now it is generally accepted that the burning was either accidental or the result of a hostile attack.

Many of the small gullies leading to the summit of the island have been blocked by small stretches of walling in order to provide additional protection for the fort.

54 Dunadd, Fort, Mid Argyll

Mid 1st millennium AD.

NR 836935. Signposted on the west side of the A 816 at a tricky bend about 1.5 km north of Kilmichael Glassary; park in the space indicated and follow the rocky path to the fort.

HBM (SDD).

The fort occupies an isolated rocky boss which rises from a flat surrounding valley that must in earlier times have been very boggy. The upper terraces of the boss are defended by four lines of walling on different levels, and, on present evidence, it seems likely that most of the visible walls date to the middle and later 1st millennium AD. The site has been excavated on no less than three occasions: in 1904, in 1929 and in 1980-81, and it is not until the results of the most recent campaign are known that a full account will be possible. The small finds from all the excavations, however, show that the site was indeed an important one in the mid 1st millennium AD, and it is thus likely that Dunadd was one of the main centres of the kingdom of Dalriada at this time.

The site is a confusing one to visit. The main approach to the lowest terrace of the fort is through a narrow rocky defile, at the end of which would have been strong wooden gates doubtless with adjoining stone or wooden towers; the wall of this lowest terrace is unusually well preserved, perhaps partly reconstructed in modern times, but the outer face on the west is still an impressive expanse of drystone construction. There is a carefully lined well near the north end of the terrace. Several rectangular foundations were discovered in the course of excavations situated to the east of the entrance, but there is as yet no dating evidence. The twin summits of the rock now beckon, but only the western summit is defended, and as the ascent is continued, a second, but very denuded line of walling is crossed.

The summit fort and a smaller walled outer work to the east are remarkable not for the preservation of their walling, but for a series of carvings on a slab of rock situated at the south-west end of the lower enclosure. Today the original carvings are covered and protected by a glass-fibre replica. Here there is the carved figure of a boar, several lines of ogam inscription, the outline of a footprint, and a hollowed-out basin. Ogam is a way of writing, of Irish origin, using groups of strokes at angles to a base-line, though at Dunadd the natural fissures in the rock have been used as a base-line. Unlike Irish ogams, however, the inscription cannot be translated, and it thus has more in common with the enigmatic inscriptions of Pictland. The boar too has aspects of decoration that might suggest a Pictish origin, but more tellingly it lacks several features that would make such an attribution positive. The basin and the footprint have been interpreted as being part of the rituals of royal inaugurations of the kings of Dalriada.

The most recent excavations have shown that there were certainly two phases of construction of the topmost fortification, but there is as yet no evidence of the date of the earlier. Most of the finds from the site belong to the 6th to 9th centuries AD, although both earlier and later finds have been recovered; some of the most important finds indicate that metal-working of a high order was being undertaken—several hundred mould fragments have been found—and many beautiful brooches must have been produced. The finds from the early excavations are displayed in RMS.

55 Dun Aisgain, Dun, Mull

Early 1st millennium AD.

NM 377452. Situated on a rocky knoll some 600 m south-west of Burg, and approached on foot from the road between Calgary and Kilninian (B 8073) from Burg.

This is an exceptionally well-preserved example from the many fine duns on Mull, set within an outer wall which clings closely to the irregular shape of the knoll. The dun itself is circular, measuring about 10.5 m in diameter within a wall up to 2.75 m in thickness on either side of the entrance. To increase the stability of the dun the wall has been built with a marked batter and in places it still stands to a height of 2.75 m. The entrance passage, on the west side, has door jambs about half-way along its length and there are traces of a bar-hole. An internal mural gallery can still be seen within the thickness of the wall, particularly on the north-east flank; this was presumably a structural feature to allow greater height to be achieved while at the same time ensuring the stability of the main elements of the wall.

Dunadd, Mid Argyll (no. 54).

56 Dun an t-Siamain, Dun, North Uist

1st millennium AD.
NF 885595. Leave the A 865 at Knockqueen and follow the track to Calternish, then walk east across the moor towards Eaval.

Dun an t-Siamain is built on a small island on the east side of Loch Dun an t-Siamain, on the west side of Eaval. Typical of many of the duns in North Uist, it is approached by a curved causeway which is still negotiable. The outer wall face of the dun rises directly from the water: it is roughly oval on plan but has an angle on the east side. The interior is obscured by fallen stones and vegetation, but the position of the entrance, just south of the causeway, can be seen, and at the southern end there is a water gate.

Dun Ardtreck, Skye (no. 58).

57 Dun an Sticir, Broch, North Uist

Later 1st millennium BC and later medieval period.
NF 897777. Readily visible from the B 893 just before reaching Newtonferry, Dun an Sticir has a complex approach: cross either of two causeways from opposite sides of the loch to an island, and thence by another causeway to the island on which the broch stands.

The entrance, with one mighty fallen lintel, faces the causeway. Part of the guard chamber can be seen to the right of the entrance, and in places the wall-faces of intramural passages are still visible.

A late rectangular building within the ruins causes some initial confusion; this may be associated with Hugh MacDonald, son of Archibald the Clerk, who is said to have survived for over a year in this refuge before being finally captured and left to die horribly in the dungeon at Duntulm Castle (no. 26).

58 Dun Ardtreck, Broch, Skye

Later 1st millennium BC.
NG 335358. Follow B 8009 through Carbost, and where it forks take the left fork for Fiscavaig; 1.3 km from the junction, there is a crossroad. Walk up the track to the right and at the end, strike off to the left, through a gate and across moorland.

Dun Ardtreck is clearly closely related to the brochs, being in effect half of a broch built on a knob of rock on the edge of a sea cliff. An arc of walling protects the landward side enclosing an area about 13 m by 10 m. The entrance is in the middle with a raised threshold, and it has the door checks and guard chamber usually found in brochs; within, there are openings to intramural galleries. At the cliff edge the walls are reduced to their lowest courses, but stand to a height of nearly 2 m in places on the landward side.

Callanish stone circle, Lewis:
aerial view (no. 76).

Callanish stone circle, Lewis (no. 76).

*Temple Wood Stone Circle,
Mid Argyll: upright stone with
part of the double spiral (no. 81).*

*Kilmichael Glassary, Cup-marked
rock Mid Argyll (no. 85).*

59 Dun Beag, Broch, Skye

Later 1st millennium BC/early
1st millennium AD.
NG 339386. Signposted on the A 863 just west
of Bracadale.
HBM (SDD).

The broch stands on the top of a knoll, readily
approached from the south-west but steeper on the
northern side. Though now truncated and cleared of
fallen stone, it still has many of the characteristic
features of its class; it measures about 11 m in
diameter within stout walls 4.3 m thick. The outer
wall-face is battered and like many of the Skye brochs,
very neatly built using square-sided facing-stones in
courses. The entrance is to the east and has door
checks to keep the wooden door in position; it is not
protected by a guard chamber at ground level, though
this is a common feature in brochs. There is a small
cell within the wall to the right of the entrance, but it is
entered from inside the broch. On the left of the
entrance is an opening leading to a neat stairway of
about twenty steps, and opposite, but above the floor
level, is another opening giving access to the
intramural galleries, which can be traced for some
distance on either side.

Dun Beag, Skye (no. 59).

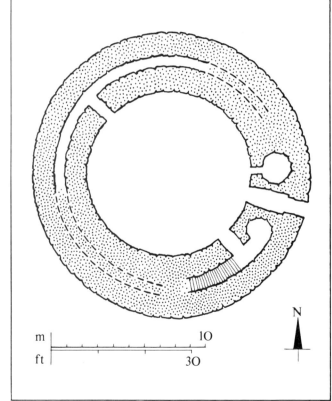

60 Dun Baravat, Broch, Bernera, Lewis
1st millennium AD.
NB 155355. Turn off the B 8011 on the Bernera road, and after crossing the bridge to the island, continue for about 1.5 km then walk westwards over the moor to Loch Baravat.

A causeway from the north shore leads to Dun Baravat, a broch-like structure on a small island. The northern section of wall is preserved to a height of just over 3 m; there is no entrance on this side. On the inner wall-face there is a scarcement and an entrance to an intramural gallery.

61 Dun Carloway, Broch, Lewis
Later 1st millennium BC/early
1st millennium AD.
NB 190413. Signposted on A 858 south of Carloway; car park.
HBM (SDD).

The broch at Carloway is one of the best preserved examples in Scotland, standing in places almost to its original height of over 9 m. Part of the wall has fallen in a way that makes it easy to appreciate the principles of broch construction. The intramural galleries are visible in the broken edges of the wall, yet enough remains to show the smooth, sloping profile of the outer wall, and the tight and neat drystone walling. The broch is situated in a good defensive position, with relatively level ground to the north and a steep fall to the south. It is built partly on bedrock: a large slab carefully positioned over an awkward outcrop provides a level footing for the outer wall, and there are also rock outcrops within the walls. The entrance is on the north side, with a guard chamber to the right, and opposite, an opening allows access to the intramural staircase which led to the upper galleries. Between the entrance and the door to the stair are low entrances to two cells within the thickness of the wall. There is a scarcement probably used to support a timber roof or possibly a first floor. The opening above the stair door may have been to let light into the galleries rather than to provide access to an upper storey. Recent excavations in one of the side cells produced pottery and hearths a little later than the

Dun Carloway, Lewis (no. 61).

main period of occupation. Evidently the defensive qualities of the broch were used in the medieval period, as the tale of a clan feud relates how Donald Cam MacAulay climbed the outer wall by inserting his knife between the stones, to throw down burning heather and thus smother a party of Morrisons, who had taken refuge within the walls after a cattle raid.

62 Dun Fiadhairt, Broch, Skye

*Later 1st millennium BC/early
1st millennium AD.*
NG 231504. Follow the A 850 for 3 km beyond Dunvegan Castle to where the road crosses a causeway between two lochs. Walk west, crossing an isthmus to the Fiadhairt peninsula, and veer to the right as you go up the slope.

This broch is well positioned on a rocky knoll with steep sides and low boggy ground to the east. There is a quantity of fallen stone both inside and outside, partly the result of excavations in 1914; but the circular shape is clear, and the cells and galleries can be seen quite easily. Measuring about 9.5 m in diameter within a wall about 3.6 m thick and standing internally to a maximum height of 2 m, this broch is unusual in having two entrances. The main entrance is on the west side, the ascent being partially channelled between parallel walls outside the main structure. There are door checks on either side of the entrance and beyond them the entrance to small guard cells, one on either side of the doorway. The second entrance, which retains some of its lintels, is directly opposite the first and is much narrower. No guard cell is apparent, although within the entrance-passage there is an opening to a long and partially lintelled gallery which occupies almost the whole of the south side of the broch. On the north side of the broch there are two openings, one to a pair of cells, the other to a short gallery, with stairs rising on the right-hand side of the doorway.

m | 5 | 10
ft | | 30

N

Dun Carloway, Lewis (no. 61)

63 Dun Hallin, Skye

*Later 1st millennium BC/early
1st millennium AD.*

NG 256592. Take the B 886 from Fairy Bridge and go through Stein to Hallin. The dun is best approached from the small road which turns right across the peninsula to Geary.

Dun Hallin, on a plateau of rock to the east of Hallin, looks over the lochs on both sides of Waternish. The circular plan is clear, and the position of the entrance and in places parts of the gallery walls are visible. There are traces of walling around the edge of the plateau on which the broch stands.

Two more brochs further north on the Waternish peninsula are worth visiting. Returning to Hallin, continue along the road to Trumpan, where in the graveyard there is an interesting carved slab representing a priest. At the bend in the road to the east of the old church, walk north along the track for about 2 km to Dun Borrafiach (NG 235637), which overlooks a broad valley. The interior is full of fallen stones, but the exterior is remarkable for the size of some of the stones used and the quality of the building. The position of the entrance and some of the gallery wall-faces can be distinguished.

About 1 km further north, again on the right of the track and up a slight rise, is Dun Gearymore (NG 236649) which is very ruinous, though most of the inner and outer wall-faces are visible, as are the walls of galleries, but not the entrance. In the north-west sector a few missing lintels give access to a gallery which is now mostly below ground level; it is low and narrow but can be traced for over 6 m round the base of the broch.

Dun Hallin, Skye (no. 63).

Dun Borrafiach, Skye (no. 63).

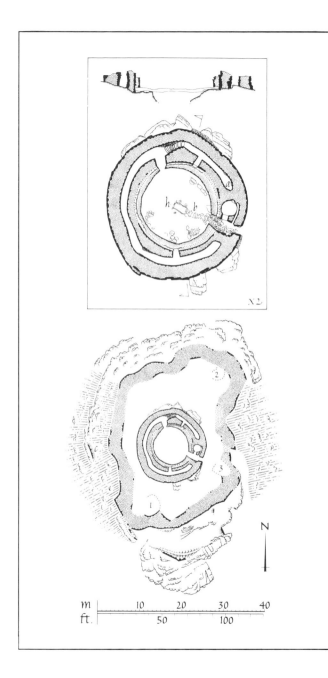

64 Dun Mor, Broch, Vaul, Tiree

Mid 1st century BC to about AD 200.
NM 042492. Situated about 300 m north-west of
Vaul.

This well-preserved broch, situated on a rocky knoll
close to the shore, was excavated between 1962 and
1964, and we thus have detailed information about the
sequence of construction and the objects discovered in
the various levels. Set within an irregular but stoutly
made outwork, it illustrates many of the features of
broch-building including a basal gallery, scarcement
ledge and guard cell. The broch measures about 9.2 m
in diameter within a wall up to 4.5 m in thickness and
surviving to a height of 2.2 m. Within the thickness of
the wall there is a gallery; the main entrance to this
was on the NNW side of the interior where there is a
doorway, which also opens onto a stairway to the
upper levels of the broch. Two smaller doorways still
lintelled by massive slabs provide additional access
from the central court into the gallery. Originally the
gallery would have been lintelled, and the broch would
have been several metres taller (perhaps as much as
8 m in all), though there is no reason to think that it
would necessarily have reached the heights of Dun
Telve, Glenelg (10 m) or Mousa in Shetland (13.3 m).

The entrance is on the ESE side of the broch; it has
checks against which a strong wooden door would
rest, the door itself swinging on a pivot-stone still
visible in the floor of the passage on the south side.
The door could be held in a closed position by a thick
wooden bar which was kept in place in twin bar-holes.
There is a guard cell on the north side of the passage,
the low lintelled doorway leading to a corbelled cell
measuring about 2 m in diameter.

The interior of the broch would probably have held a
range of timber buildings supported by upright posts
and by horizontal members, which rested against the

133

scarcement ledge visible on the inner face of the wall at a height of about 1.4 m. In a secondary phase the internal arrangements of the broch were radically altered and non-defensive occupation has been envisaged, with the broch walls lowered in height and some of the stone used to provide an additional internal line of walling, which seals off two of the three entrances into the mural gallery.

The original building of the broch probably dates to about the middle of the first century BC with its reconstruction as a non-defensive round-house perhaps about AD 200; the ruins of the broch tower remained the focus for intermittent settlement or shelter in the following centuries, including the Viking Age as is proved by the discovery of a composite bone comb of Norse type. The finds are displayed in the Hunterian Museum, University of Glasgow.

Dun Nosebridge, Islay (no. 65).

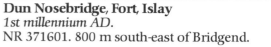

65 Dun Nosebridge, Fort, Islay
1st millennium AD.
NR 371601. 800 m south-east of Bridgend.

Situated on an isolated grass-covered ridge, this fort is one of the most unusual in the west of Scotland, and its date is quite unknown. The main defence is a wall which appears to enclose the summit of the ridge (perhaps 25 m by 15 m). Two outer works partly enclose the fort at lower levels and both include material which has been quarried from ditches on either side. Such a technique, together with the almost rectangular plan of the fort, draws it apart from most of the iron-age defences in the area. In the absence of excavation, however, the date of the fort is uncertain; both the commanding position and the preservation of the various components make this a rewarding site to visit and puzzle over.

The only comparable site on Islay, Dun Guaire (NR 389648), situated about 500 m SSW of Kilmeny farm, is less well preserved.

66 Dun Ringill, Dun, Skye
Later centuries BC/early centuries AD.
NG 561170. Take the A 881 towards Elgol, but just beyond Kirkibost, stop near the top of the hill above the bridge, and walk along a track through a field, skirting the corner of the forestry plantation to follow the track into the woods beside the river and on to the shore of Loch Slapin; continue north along the shore.

Dun Ringill is built on the edge of a low cliff on the west shore of Loch Slapin. On either side there are steep-sided inlets so that it is readily approached only from the west, and the entrance is on this side. Though now ruinous and overgrown, the thick walls of this oval dun can be seen clearly on the landward side, enclosing an area about 17.5 m by 22 m, and the long narrow entrance appears to have been the only way in. There are door checks and bar-holes in the entrance passage, which retains several of its lintels, and has more than one phase of building. Within, there is a mass of tumbled stone, but much of the line of the inner wall-face can be seen; it has three openings in it, one of them leading to the remains of a large cell on the south side. The ruined rectangular building on the seaward side is of later date.

67 Kildonan, Dun, Kintyre

Early to mid 1st millennium AD.
NR 780277. Ready access across a stile from a small Forestry Commission car park: the dun is situated on a rocky bluff between the road from Campbeltown to Carradale and the sea, 3.5 km south of Saddell.

This D-shaped dun is exceptionally well preserved with the outer and inner face surviving to a height of over 2 m externally. The shape of the dun, which measures about 19 m by 13 m internally, is partly dictated by the rock stack on which it was built; its preservation is due, at least in part, to the use of an inner revetment within the wall (an inward facing slab construction) still visible in several places. The main features of interest are the entrance, a double staircase

within the wall and a cell within the wall on the north-east side. The impressive entrance has door checks, against which a stout timber door might be placed, and bar-slots to accommodate the beam to keep the door in position. The wall to the south-east of the entrance is in two distinct thicknesses, doubtless a device to improve the stability of the dun. On the west side of the wall the twin flights of steps provide access to the wall head. On the north-east side there is a small cell within the thickness of the wall.

Excavations between 1936 and 1938 and again in 1984 have revealed a rich assemblage of finds including

pottery and metalwork indicating three periods of occupation: the construction of the dun in the 1st or 2nd century AD; its re-use, coupled probably with re-building, in about the 9th century AD; there was finally a re-occupation between the late 12th and early 14th century AD.

68 Leccamore, Dun, Luing

Early 1st millennium AD.
NM 750107. On the island of Luing, follow the road from the ferry for 4.5 km, take the track to Leccamore farm for permission; the dun is 500 m south-west of the farm.

This dun is both remarkably well preserved and also contains several unusual features. Situated on the summit of a long ridge, it has been defended both by an outer wall and on the north by two rock-cut ditches which run athwart the ridge. The dun measures about 20 m by 13 m within a wall which is up to 5 m in thickness. The dun has two apparently contemporary entrances, one on the south-west and the other on the north-east side. The outer wall-face on the south-west has been particularly carefully constructed with a distinct batter, and the walls of the entrance passage still stand to a height of almost 2 m. The passage has door jambs close to the outside, one of the jamb-stones bearing at least fifteen cup-markings on one face; perhaps the stone was one slab of a cist burial discovered in the course of the original building work. The bar-hole and the opposing slot for storing the bar when the door was open are still visible, the slot extending for a distance of 2.7 m into the thickness of the wall. The north-east entrance is less well preserved, but there are cells on both sides of the passage, that on the north-west side being carefully corbelled. Leading from the west side of this cell there is a flight of steps, which presumably allowed easy access to the wall-head in times of attack.

69 Tirefour, Broch, Lismore

Later 1st millennium BC.

NM 867429. Situated 4 km from the jetty for the Port Appin ferry; 3 km from the jetty take the track on the left to Balure.

The magnificent broch of Tirefour stands on the highest part of a ridge on the east coast of the island, a position that offers commanding views of the surrounding seascapes. The broch is circular on plan with the central courtyard measuring about 12 m within a massive wall about 4.5 m thick and still 5 m in height. The entrance is on the south-west flank. The wall has been constructed in such a way that the basal part is solid rather than hollow; at a height of about 2.5 m there are traces of an internal gallery, and it is likely that the upper part of the broch was of classic hollow-wall construction. At a height of about 2.5 m from the original internal floor-level, there is a distinct scarcement or ledge 0.6 m wide, which would have allowed internal timber buildings or floors to be keyed into the stone structure of the tower; no excavation has been undertaken and thus we do not know about any internal post-holes which might help to reconstruct such buildings more positively. Look out for the traces of two outer walls, now much denuded, which have provided additional protection for the broch on the north-east and south-west flanks.

Tirefour Broch, Lismore (no. 69).

CAIRNS

Most of the round cairns we see today were designed to cover burials contained in small stone coffins or 'cists'; most burials of this type belong to the first half of the second millennium BC, though earlier and later examples are known, and several occur in small groups or cemeteries, sometimes apparently in a linear arrangement with one cairn heading a line of later examples. Many of those marked on the OS maps, however, are merely large mounds of stones like Corriechrevie, Kintyre (NR 738540), and Kilmartin Glebe Cairn (no. 71), and, however interesting their excavation may be to the archaeologist, they have little to offer the visitor. The Kilmartin sites are among the most interesting and several have been displayed to reveal their burial-cists. Some demonstrate the carpentry as well as stone-working skills of their builders: cists at Ri Cruin for example (no. 73) show a knowledge of the woodworking technique of tongue-and-groove, for the side-slabs have carefully pecked out grooves, which were designed to allow the end-slabs to slot easily into position. Similar construction has been found in the Isle of Scilly and Brittany, illustrating the far flung contacts of metal-using communities, but also hinting at the range of techniques available to the builders of timber houses. For although the monuments relating to ritual and death survive, we have little indication of the houses of the living.

Much of the dating evidence for this period comes from radiocarbon analyses of the organic remains (usually bones or charcoal) from burials, but the accompanying gravegoods also help to build up a picture of the various contacts between different areas. Several pottery types are mentioned here; Beaker pottery, found in chambered tombs (nos 86-87, 89-90), belongs to a long-lived type with several styles, some with continental parallels, other of highly-developed local groups. Food Vessels are highly ornamented pots, often bowls, which appear to be of rather later, but overlapping, date.

Steinacleit, Shader, Lewis (no. 74).

70 Dunchragaig, Cairn, Mid Argyll

2nd millennium BC.
NR 853968. Signposted on the A 816, about 2 km south of Kilmartin; there is a car park on the opposite side of the road.
HBM (SDD).

The large cairn of water-worn boulders is over 30 m in diameter and is still over 2 m high. It has been subjected to excavation on at least three occasions, latterly by J H Craw in 1929 and the stones are now rather spread. Two cists are still visible; in 1864 on the SE perimeter Canon Greenwell, famous for his exploration of prehistoric tombs in the north of England, found a chamber of unusual boulder construction, measuring 2.6 m in length by about 1 m in both width and height, with a massive capstone 4.2 m long and 2.5 m broad. The cist contained several burials, but no gravegoods; cremated bones of up to ten individuals being found at one end and an inhumation at the centre. The cist still visible at the centre of the site is at a high level within the cairn material and is thus probably not the primary burial; it contained a fine Food Vessel (now in RMS), cremated bones and flint fragments. A further cist (not now visible) was found to the E of the centre; its contents were similar. Even in its ruined state the cairn illustrates the large number of burials that might be inserted into such a mound over what may have been a long period of time.

71 Glebe Cairn, Kilmartin, Mid Argyll

2nd millennium BC.
NR 833989. Park at the petrol station just to the north of Kilmartin village and follow the signposted access across the adjacent field.
HBM (SDD).

Now a massive pile of stones some 33.5 m in diameter and 4 m in height, with no other distinguishing features, this cairn is the northernmost of the line on the valley floor. The cairn covered several burial deposits and may have been the result of building and rebuilding over several centuries. One cist contained an inhumation burial with a Food Vessel as well as the beads of a jet necklace. The central cist, which was constructed in a shaft, contained an inhumation burial and another Food Vessel.

72 Nether Largie, Mid and North Cairns, Mid Argyll

2nd millennium BC.
NR 830983 and NR 830984. 800 m SSE of Kilmartin village turn west over a small bridge, follow the road for 350 m, then park in the space indicated.
Mid Cairn is 300 m to the NNE along the track; North Cairn is 150 m further on.
HBM (SDD).

Nether Largie Mid Cairn is both ruinous and unhelpfully displayed; it is about 30 m in diameter within a kerb of big stones, but excavation-debris masks much of the perimeter. Two cists were found when the cairn was excavated in 1929. That on the north, its position now indicated by four concrete posts, was empty; its side-slabs had carefully grooved slots into which the end-slabs had been placed. The southern cist is still visible, its capstone supported on steel bars to allow the interior to be seen, but it too was empty when excavated. There is a single cup-mark and axe-marking on its north-west end-slab.

Nether Largie North cairn is an impressive, though largely reconstructed, bowl-shaped mound about 20 m in diameter and 3 m in height; a cist at its centre is approached through a hatch with steps down into a viewing chamber. The cist is 1.6 m by 0.65 m and about 0.6 m deep, but, when excavated in 1930, only one tooth, a few fragments of charcoal and a little ochre were found. What is remarkable about the cist, however, is that two of the slabs have been carefully decorated: one end-slab has representations of two distinctive axe-heads, while on the underside of the capstone there are at least ten axe-heads and about forty cup-markings; it is likely that the cup-markings were the earliest decoration on the slab, for some of them seem to have been made shallower by the carving of the axes.

73 Ri Cruin, Cairn, Mid Argyll
2nd millennium BC.
NR 825971. Take the south-east fork to the south of Temple Wood (no. 81); the path to Ri Cruin is 350 m on the south side of the road. Signposted. HBM (SDD).

This cairn is now very much reduced in height, but its diameter of about 20 m is probably close to its original extent. Excavated on two occasions, by Dean Mapleton in 1870 and J H Craw in 1929, three cists were discovered, all without gravegoods; but all have interesting features about their construction: that to the north of the centre, which was covered by a massive slab and contained a cremation deposit, is grooved and rebated at one end to give the end-slab a tighter fit; both cists to the south of the centre have grooved and rebated slabs. The west

end-slab of the southernmost cist has been decorated with seven pecked axe-markings. The narrow vertically placed slab at the east end is a replacement for a further decorated slab, which bore a long pecked groove with short pecked lines at right angles to it; the original stone was sadly destroyed in a fire, but there is a cast in RMS.

74 Steinacleit, Shader, Lewis
3rd or 2nd millennium BC.
NB 396540. Signposted on the A 857 in Lower Shader. HBM (SDD).

Once thought to be the remains of a chambered cairn, this monument is now considered to be a domestic settlement. A circular structure, some 16 m in diameter, may have been a house, with massive stones used in its wall; it lies to one side of an oval enclosure marked out by a low wall, on a gentle slope above a small loch. Without excavation, neither date nor function can be certain. A standing stone, Clach Stei Lin, is situated about 165 m to the north, and Clach an Trushal (no. 77) is visible in the distance to the west.

Ri Cruin, Cairn, Mid Argyll: axe markings south cist (no. 73)

139

STANDING STONES AND STONE CIRCLES

Many standing stones are shown on Ordnance Survey maps, perhaps indicating routes, boundaries or burials; for many stones an astronomical significance has also been proposed, relying on a far notch on the horizon as the other end of the line of observation of some lunar or solsticial event. Such interpretations have been criticised because of the multiplicity of possible horizon-markers, but they hold an irresistible fascination, linking little understood monuments such as standing stones, alignments and circles with both modern astronomical and scientific ideals. At one extreme the visitor can see a standing stone and marvel at the skills of early man in setting it up; at the other he can conjure up the prehistoric equivalent of today's silicon chip. The archaeologist has no solution, and we offer a small number of exciting stones to visit as examples of one of the least understood classes of prehistoric monument: Ballinaby (no. 75) and Clach an Trushal (no. 77), as large stones; Diarmid's Pillar, Strontoiller (no. 80), because of its folklore and its characteristic association with a kerb-cairn; the linear settings such as Dervaig (no. 78) as examples of the more complex arrangements of stones, such as Ballymeanoch (NR 833964) and Nether Largie (NR 827977), which can only be seen from the road because there is no public access. Callanish (no. 76), the most exceptional prehistoric monument in the west of Scotland, incorporates many of these features. Stone circles, however, are rare; several are poorly preserved, for example an unusual pair at Hough, on Tiree (NL 958451) and a partly excavated circle at Cultoon on Islay (NR 195569). Apart from Callanish, the best preserved include Lochbuie, Mull (no. 79), Ettrick Bay on Bute (NS 044667), and Pobull Fhinn on North Uist (NF 842650; see no. 86).

Callanish Stone Circle, Lewis: main avenue (no. 76).

75 Ballinaby, Standing Stones, Islay

2nd millennium BC.

NR 219672 and NR 221673. Approach is by foot from Ballinaby farm, to the north of Loch Gorm to the north of the Rinns of Islay.

One of the most impressive standing stones in the west of Scotland is situated in a prominent position and despite its thinness can be seen from considerable distances. The stone is almost 5 m in height, but is as little as 0.3 m thick at the base. The second stone, 200 m to the north, has been damaged by stone-breaking and is now only 2 m high.

---

76 Callanish, Stone Circles and Standing Stones, Lewis

3rd and early 2nd millennium BC.

NB 213330. Signposted, on a loop road off the A 858. It is probably best to approach the site by taking the more northerly route, which goes through Callanish village, thus avoiding driving up a steep and twisting single track road. Two other circles nearby, at NB 225327 and NB 229304, are also signposted.
HBM (SDD).

The main site stands on the southern end of a ridge of rock, on the east shore of Loch Roag. It is visible from a considerable distance in some directions and is particularly impressive when seen against the skyline.

The plan is unique: a circle of standing stones, with an avenue, or double line, of stones to the north, and, to the south, east and west, single lines of stones. Most are slabs of Lewisian gneiss, set with their long axes on the line of the setting of which they form part. Thirteen stones, up to 3.5 m in height, form a circle just over 5 m in diameter, with a tall central monolith standing to a height of 4.75 m. To the north, lines of ten and nine stones form the west and east sides of an avenue about 82 m long. The spacing and height of these stones is irregular; there are long gaps at the northern end, but the northernmost stones of each line may mark the original end of the avenue, particularly as one is squarish in section and the other stands at right angles to the line. The western line contains four stones and the eastern five, the outermost recently raised from beneath its covering of peat and replaced upright in its original socket. The southern line also contains five stones, and close to the circle there is an extra stone to east and west of this line; the eastern one was placed there in the nineteenth century and may not be part of the original plan. The southern line of stones is almost precisely on a north-south line, but the other lines and the avenue do not mark true cardinal points in relation to the circle.

Until the mid-19th century a thick growth of peat partially covered the stones and the lower parts of some of them are still slightly paler as a result of this. The peat was stripped by Sir James Matheson, proprietor of the island, in 1857, revealing the remains of a small circular chambered cairn within the eastern half of the circle. Several kerb-stones are still visible, and two stones of the circle on the east side are also incorporated on either side of the entrance passage; the central monolith stands within the western edge of the cairn. The entrance passage is on the east side, and both it and the chamber are mainly of drystone construction, though the chamber has portal stones, and a further two upright slabs divide it into two compartments. Minute fragments of bone, assumed to be human, were found in the chamber, but the tomb must have been robbed in antiquity before it was completely covered by peat.

A large oval heap of stones to the south-west of the circle, near the perimeter fence, bears a superficial resemblance to a chambered cairn; it is, however, related to the hamlet that formerly stood near the monument and is almost certainly a corn-drying kiln.

Callanish Stone Circle, Lewis:
central circle and cairn (no. 76).

142

double circle, the inner represented by four standing stones, and the outer by eight standing stones as well as five which have fallen.

Another circle, known as Garynahine or Ceann Hulavig (Callanish IV) can be seen to the west of the Uig road (B 8011) on a hill about 1.5 km south of Garynahine Lodge. Five impressive stones form an oval (13 m by 9 m); the centre has been excavated and appears to contain an upright stone surrounded by a small cairn.

Clach an Trushal, Lewis (no. 77).

---

77 Clach an Trushal, Standing Stone, Lewis

3rd or 2nd millennium BC.
NB 375537. Take the main Ballantrushal township road west from the A 857, and then a track to the left just before the last few houses.

Reputed to mark the site of a battle, Clach an Trushal is an impressive standing stone, nearly 6 m high, leaning slightly to the south. An early 19th century print shows several feet of peat being cut away from around the base, but no archaeological discoveries were reported at this time.

---

78 Dervaig, Standing Stones, Mull

2nd millennium BC.
NM 435530. In a forestry plantation 1 km NNE of Dervaig.

The circle with its associated lines of stones is the most imposing of a group of circles at the head of Loch Roag. The circle known as Cnoc Ceann a' Gharaidh (Callanish II) is situated at the end of a track near the south end of the Callanish loop road; this is an ellipse of seven stones, two of which are prostrate, with a ruined cairn near the centre. The circle known as Cnoc Fillibhir (Callanish III) is visible from the A 858 to the south-east of the main circle. Access is by wooden steps over the fence. This appears to have been a

Linear settings of standing stones were clearly an important feature of bronze-age religious or ceremonial occasions, providing perhaps a framework for a series of rituals. One of the best-preserved linear settings is in a clearing in a forestry plantation, a position that precludes our appreciation of its situation in the landscape. Three stones are still upright, but the fourth at the north end of the group has now fallen. The three upright stones are all substantial blocks over 2 m in height.

Two other linear settings are less well-preserved or less impressive, but are more accessible. To the north of the road from Tobermory to Dervaig at a point about 850 m east of the village, an opening in the forestry fence allows access to a group of five stones of which two are still standing (NM 439520). At a point some 400 m to the south there are three other stones, one of which now forms part of a wall (NM 438516).

79 Lochbuie, Stone Circle, Mull

2nd millennium BC.
NM 617251. Situated in level parkland 300 m north of Lochbuie House.

This is one of the rare stone circles in the west of Scotland and one of the earliest monuments at the head of Loch Buie; its location underlines the attraction of the bay to early man as well as to the builders of the medieval castle and the later mansion house. The circle was originally of nine stones, but one has since been destroyed and has been replaced by an erratic boulder. The stones are up to 1.75 m in height and are associated with three outlying monoliths, one of which is 3 m in height.

Lochbuie Stone Circle, Mull (no. 79).

80 Strontoiller, Standing Stone, Cairn and Stone Circle, Lorn
2nd millennium BC.
NM 907289. The first two are situated immediately to the north of the public road through Glen Lonan, about 5 km west of Oban; the stone circle is approached from the farm track to the north of the road; there is a stile.

The stone is one of the most impressive single monoliths in Argyll, standing to height of 4 m and measuring 1.2 m by 0.9 m at the base. Tradition has it that the stone, Clach na Carraig or Clach Diarmid, and the little cairn to the south-east mark the burial place of the Irish hero Diarmid. The cairn, which is about 4.5 m in overall diameter, has a kerb of large granite boulders; excavation in 1967 discovered only a small quantity of cremated bones and white quartz pebbles around the bases of all the kerb-stones. There are very few stone circles in Argyll, and that at Strontoiller is one of the more accessible, although the stones are not individually large. There are about thirty-one boulders set on a 'circle' of about 20 m in diameter.

These three sites, together with a series of cairns at the southern end of Loch Nell, 3.5 km to the south-west, suggest that this has been an important area of settlement in the neolithic and bronze ages.

81 Temple Wood, Stone Circles, Mid Argyll
2nd and 3rd millennia BC.
NR 826978. To the west of the road between Kilmartin School, Nether Largie, and Poltalloch. HBM (SDD).

Many of the elements of this pair of sites join to make them unusual and in so doing remind us that the groups, categories or 'norms' of the archaeological record are to some extent illusions. To the north-east there is a stone circle which was discovered in the course of recent excavations; measuring about 10.5 m by 10 m, this site was of two periods: a timber circle, the posts of which have been marked by round concrete pillars, and a stone circle, most of the uprights of which were subsequently removed, but one remains *in situ*. A radiocarbon date shows that this is one of the earliest circles in Scotland.

The sequence of construction of the larger and better known circle has been made much clearer as a result of excavation and is explained on information-panels on site. The circle of upright stones, about 12.2 m in diameter, was the architectural focus for burials over many centuries with several periods of reconstruction. As displayed today the site shows the last phase of rebuilding, when it was largely covered by a stone cairn, though some of the capping may be comparatively recent. One small cairn, built immediately outside the circle to the north-east, contained a cist with a Beaker vessel associated with three flint arrowheads and a flint scraper, but there were no burial remains. This cairn, like a second, which covered an empty cist (presumably also an unaccompanied inhumation burial), is now sealed by the bank of cairn material outside the stone circle.

Excavation in 1929 revealed that the cist at the centre of the circle had already been rifled, and thus its chronological position is uncertain; the kerb-stones of the cairn that enclosed it were, however, later destroyed, and the present stones are largely reconstructions. The cist is a well-built one, measuring 1.4 m by 0.8 m and 0.5 m in depth, and is comparable in size to several in the adjacent monuments.

One of the most unusual features of the stone circle is the presence of a pecked double spiral on one of the stones, one half on one side and the other on the next face; it is unlikely that this carving is of two periods as has sometimes been suggested.

Strontoiller, Cairn and Standing Stone, Lorn (no. 80).

Temple Wood, Stone Circle, Mid Argyll (no. 81).

CUP-AND-RING MARKINGS

Many natural outcrops of rock in Argyll are decorated with expanses of pecked cup-and-ring and cup-markings; they include some of the most impressive group of such bronze-age art to be seen in Britain, with many cups surrounded by multiple rings, often carpeting the natural rock surface with different patterns of the cup-and-ring motif. Standing stones were also decorated, including one at Temple Wood (no. 81) where there is a spiral motif; burial cists also have slabs decorated with cup-markings and in rare cases axes (nos 72-73). Many of the sheets of rock art are best visited in a late afternoon sun when a cross-light helps to pick out these enigmatic carvings. Among other extensive, but less accessible, cup-and-ring marked rock surfaces, one of the most spectacular is that at Ormaig, where there are several unusual ringed-rosette motifs (NM 822026).

Achnabreck Cup-marked rocks, Mid Argyll (no. 82).

82 Achnabreck, Cup-marked rocks, Mid Argyll
2nd millennium BC.
NR 855906. The road to Achnabreck farm itself is not signposted, but leave the A 816 between Lochgilphead and Cairnbaan 1.75 km NNW of Lochgilphead (NR 851897), follow the farm road and park in the space indicated; follow the signposted footpath behind the farm, finally crossing a large pasture field by the route indicated. The extensive sheets of cup-and-ring markings are in two fenced enclosures, the first at the edge of a pine forest and the second within the forest, some 140 m to the east, along a well-marked path.
HBM (SDD).

The rock sheets offer one of the most extensive displays of such carvings in Britain, with a bewildering profusion of multiple ring-markings, cups and grooves. On the first rock sheet there are over fifty cup-and-ring markings and many plain cup-markings, some of them unusually large; several of the figures are linked by grooves and many have grooves which run from the central cup. But it is the profusion of rings that is so striking. Up to nine rings surrounding the central cup have been counted; not all are circular, flattened sides are not uncommon. An early evening cross-light helps to capture both the decoration and the attractive colour of the rock.

At a distance of 30 m to the north-west, the second area of carving has one of the largest cup-and-ring markings so far recorded, which measures almost 1 m in overall diameter; seven rings surround a cup from which there are also two grooves.

The carvings on the highest part of the rock are not always easy to see, depending on lighting conditions, but contain some of the most unusual on the rock surface. Here, apart from cup-and-ring markings, there are double and triple-spiral motifs. It is possible that even further expanses of markings exist under the turf and heather, but in all cases where the markings are

Achnabreck Cup-marked rocks, Mid Argyll (no. 82).

currently visible, they do not appear to extend under the turf.

The second fenced enclosure contains a densely-packed series of markings, many of the cup-and-rings joined by grooves to create patterns not unlike model railway networks. The rings are less regular than those of the larger rock-sheet, several figures containing more than one cup within the encircling rings.

Probably more has been written about the 'purpose' of such markings than any other archaeological imponderable; one view quoted by Sir James Young Simpson was that 'these circles are similar to those used in astronomical plates for elucidating the revolution of the planets round the sun'. Primitive calendars, maps of villages and acts of penance have all been suggested; whatever the reason, the social or religious pressures to continue what is a rather limited 'art-form' were clearly considerable.

83 Ballygowan, Cup-marked rock, Mid Argyll
2nd millennium BC.
NR 816977. Because there is no suitable parking space, the best approach is on foot, following the track that enters the Poltalloch policies at NR 822977, turning north after 800 m and following the track till the final bend with Ballygowan in sight; the cup-marks are across the wall in a fenced enclosure 100 m to the NNW of the bend.
HBM (SDD).

Although the decorated rock surface is not as large as some of the others in the area, measuring about 2.5 m by 2 m, the markings are particularly well preserved, and the view over the valley is an extensive one. There are eleven cup-and-ring markings, with up to three rings, and at least sixty cup-markings. Several of the cup-and-ring markings have tangential grooves and there is one unusual horse-shoe carving.

84 Cairnbaan, Cup-marked rocks, Mid Argyll

2nd millennium BC.
NR 838910. The rock sheets are most readily approached by a signposted path that leads from the angle of two low modern blocks of the Cairnbaan Motor Inn.
HBM (SDD).

The two rocks are extensively decorated with cup-markings, many with encircling rings with distinct grooves; several cups are enclosed within larger ovals. The first sheet is within a fenced enclosure on the east side of a wall, the second is on the other side of the wall about 100 m to the west. The second sheet contains a profusion of cup-and-ring markings in several cases with four encircling rings, and the figures arranged in butting groups. The markings are particularly crisp in late afternoon sunlight, a time when the views across the Crinan canal and down to Lochgilphead are also impressive.

85 Kilmichael Glassary, Cup-marked rock, Mid Argyll

2nd millennium BC.
NR 857934. In a fenced enclosure in the village of Kilmichael Glassary; signposted.
HBM (SDD).

A large area of rock has been cleared of turf to reveal an expanse of cup-markings, several of them unusually large. Many of the cups have grooves, while others are at least partly surrounded by an outer ring.

Cairnbaan Cup-marked rocks, Mid Argyll (no. 84).

148

CHAMBERED CAIRNS

The communal burial places of the earliest agricultural communities of the west are among the most sophisticated examples of prehistoric architecture of early Scotland. The main burial chambers were often constructed of massive slabs and were designed so that these formed the core or chamber over which a massive cairn of stones was piled. The chambers, like family burial vaults, had to remain accessible after their initial building so that later burials might be added to the tomb, and earlier burials pushed perhaps to one side or even cleared out. Thus the tombs were either to one end of the covering cairn or entered along a narrow passage. Recent excavation in other areas has shown something of the burial rituals involved and the accompanying gravegoods—pottery, animal bones, birds and even perhaps sackfuls of fish! The tombs are the earliest public monuments in Scotland and were in use in the fourth and third millennia BC.

The chambered cairns of the west belong to two main types: passage-graves and Clyde cairns, suggesting either settlement from two rather different areas, or influence of two distinct social or religious traditions. Passage-graves comprise a simple chamber, usually round or oval, which is entered along a passage from the outside of the cairn (eg no. 90). The chambers of the Clyde group are rectangular, built of massive uprights, and divided into compartments by cross-slabs, which also have a role in supporting the side-slabs (eg no. 89). In both cases the junction of the passage or the chamber and the edge of the surrounding cairn was frequently made more impressive with the addition of upright stones to form a façade or concave forecourt, which doubtless formed the backcloth to the ceremonials of burial. Although now largely roofless, the tombs must have been incredibly dark and claustrophobic, and the complex rituals of deposition of burials that have been recorded by excavation must have been difficult to carry out in such conditions. The distribution of the two types of tomb is striking: passage-graves are only rarely found to the south of Ardnamurchan, and Clyde tombs are almost unknown to the north; Clettraval (no. 87), is one of the few exceptions.

In the Hebrides, the word 'Barp' indicates a burial cairn. Those included in this volume are some of the best; but there are others which are conspicuous heaps of stones, some having kerb-stones still visible in places, and some also with large slabs exposed which may be derived from the chamber or passage.

In Skye, impressive cairns can be seen from the road at Vatten (NG 298439 and 297440), at Broadford (NG 641237) and at Kensaleyre (NG 420513) where the cairn is some distance from the road on the flood plain of the river Haultin. The remains of a cairn, including some large stones which must have been part of the chamber, can be seen on the west side of the road which forms a loop to Ullinish, off the A 863 (NG 323379).

North Uist is particularly well endowed with cairns; there are long ones such as Barpa nam Feannag (NF 856720) and Caravat Barp (NF 836603) easily visible from the A 865 between Carinish and the North Ford causeway. The round cairn of Tigh Cloiche Mharrogh (NF 833695) can be seen from Barpa Langass (no. 86).

A round cairn on the north slope of Reineval, South Uist (NF 754259) can be reached by following a track from Milton.

In Lewis the round cairn of Carn a' Mharc (NB 472438) can be found by following a track from Gress, and large stones representing a chamber and possibly kerb-stones can be seen at Garrabost (NB 523330).

86 Barpa Langass, Chambered Cairn, North Uist
3rd millennium BC.
NF 837657. Barpa Langass is on the A 867 between Clachan and Lochmaddy, just north of the turn to Langass and clearly visible from the road.

Barpa Langass, a large cairn some 25 m in diameter and 4 m in height, on the western slopes of Ben Langass, is immediately obvious to anyone passing along the Lochmaddy-Clachan road; a passage-grave, it is the only chambered cairn in the Western Isles which is known to retain its chamber intact. Kerb-stones may still be seen in places around the circular cairn, especially on the northern side, and the line of stones forming the north side of the forecourt is still visible. The passage itself is about 4 m long; some of the lintels are missing from the outer end, which is partially blocked by fallen stones. The walls are formed by large slabs with some drystone walling above. At the inner end, a tall stone supporting a broken roofing slab partially blocks the passage. The chamber is oval on plan, measuring 4 m by 1.8 m, and is formed of very large upright slabs with drystone walling between and above them. Excavation in the early years of this century produced some sherds of beaker pottery, a flint arrowhead and flakes as well as burnt bones.

Walk south-east for 1 km or directly east to the top of Ben Langass and then south down the hill towards the loch to find the stone 'circle' Pobull Fhinn (NF 842650). The monument may also be approached by following the track to Langass Lodge and continuing along the slope on much the same line.

Pobull Fhinn, on the southern slopes of Ben Langass, is an oval setting of irregular shaped stones, enclosing an area which has been partially terraced; the slope is cut into on the uphill side and possibly built up a little on the downhill side.

Barpa Langass, Chambered Cairn, North Uist (no. 86).

87 Clettraval, Chambered Cairn, North Uist

3rd millennium BC.

NF 749713. Leave the A 865 opposite the turn to Tigharry, on a private track which skirts the north end of Loch Eaval before climbing the hill South Clettraval to the radar station on top.

Although the cairn at Clettraval is a long wedge shape, it has suffered severely from robbing, and the original outline is no longer visible; its chamber, however, belongs to the Clyde type and it is thus unique in the Western Isles. At the east end, slabs forming the façade are visible, mainly on the south side of the chamber, where a line of five is conspicuous, now slightly displaced from their true positions. Some kerb-stones can also be seen on the south side of the cairn. Most of the large slabs of the chamber walls also remain, set in overlapping pairs, so that the faces of the chamber walls are not straight, but stepped, rather like the sections of a telescope. There are sill-slabs across the chamber at the junction of each pair of stones. At the west end are two upright slabs, which are the remains of the end compartment. A large quantity of neolithic and Beaker pottery, now in NMAS, was found when the cairn was excavated in 1934, but only a few pieces of burnt bone survived of the burial deposits.

Immediately to the west of this, and at a lower level, is the site of a circular house of iron-age date; the inner wall face can be clearly seen in its northern half, though obscured by fallen stones on the south side; also in the northern half can be seen several radial walls, like the spokes of a wheel, but the central area was left open. 'Wheelhouses' such as this are not uncommon in the Uists and Barra, although few are visible above ground.

Barpa Langass, Chambered Cairn, North Uist: plan (no. 86)

88 Dun Bharpa, Chambered Cairn, Barra

3rd millennium BC.

NF 671019. The site can be approached from the northern Borve road, turning off the A 888. The cairn stands in the saddle between two hills, dominating the view to north and south.

Little stone has been removed from the cairn, although the chamber has probably been entered in recent times from the top. A number of large slabs are set near the edge of the cairn, and other slabs on the eastern side show where the passage runs and probably the position of the chamber; a very large slab lying flat on the top of the cairn may well be a capstone of the chamber. The commanding position is probably responsible for the name 'Dun', although the early identification of the site as a burial cairn is recognised in the second element of the name.

151

Nether Largie, South, Chambered Cairn, Mid Argyll: interior of chamber (no. 89).

89 Nether Largie South, Chambered Cairn, Mid Argyll

3rd and 2nd millennia BC.
NR 828979. About 1 km south-west of Kilmartin village; signposted (see no. 72).
HBM (SDD).

This cairn was probably the oldest of the series of burial sites that form the linear cemetery at Kilmartin; it contained a well-preserved chamber of Clyde type, the customary tomb-architecture of the neolithic inhabitants of Argyll, as well as two individual cists, only one of which is still visible. The chamber is now

at the centre of a large cairn measuring about 40 m in overall diameter, but it is likely that the final shape of the cairn owes more to its reconstruction when the bronze-age cists were added than to the original intentions of the neolithic builders. The cairn was most probably trapezoidal with the straight sides now masked by the addition of further stones. The chamber is oblong on plan, measuring 6 m in length and up to 1.2 m in width, and is divided by transverse slabs into four compartments. The massive slabs of the eastern side of the chamber, supplemented by drystone walling, appear to be original; the western side is at least in part reconstructed. The slabs of the roof may also have been replaced. There are two transverse slabs at the entrance as well as a pair of blocking stones. Entry is now made by going across the cairn and then dropping down over these blocking slabs; but when the tomb was in use there would probably have been no cairn material in front of the tomb and there may have been an impressive façade or forecourt formed by upright slabs leading straight into the chamber.

It is known from excavations carried out by Canon Greenwell in 1864 that the floor level of the chamber was about 0.6 m below the present layer of gravel, and that the transverse slabs would thus have been a much more dominant feature of the interior of the tomb.

The innermost pair of compartments was found to be paved with small pebbles, which were covered with an earthy layer containing cremated bone, a round-based neolithic vessel and quartz chips; in the inner compartment there was a small cist above the earthy layer. The cist itself was empty, but the excavator found parts of several Beakers, and inhumation burials were found nearby. In the other compartments there was only stone and rubble.

Of the two cists, both of which had been found before Greenwell's excavation, only that to the south-west of the chamber can still be seen, but nothing is known

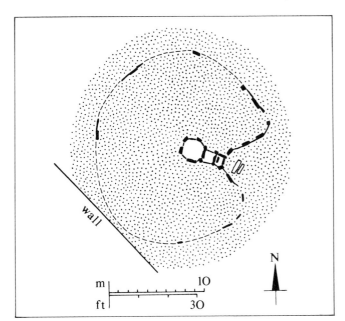

Rudh an Dunain, Chambered
Cairn, Skye: plan (no. 90)

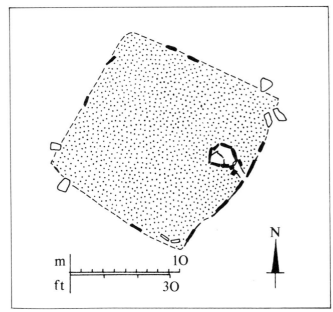

Unival, Chambered Cairn, North
Uist: plan (no. 91)

about its original contents. On the north side of the
chamber there was a second cist which contained a
fine Food Vessel, but there appears to have been no
trace of any burial remains. It is suggested that the
shape of the cairn was changed as a result of the
addition of these two cist burials over a thousand years
after the building of the chamber.

The finds from the excavation are in the British
Museum, London.

90 Rubh' an Dunain, Chambered Cairn, Skye

3rd and early 2nd millennia BC.
NG 393163. Turn off the B 8009 at Merkadale, on
the road signposted to Glenbrittle. Follow this
down to the east corner of the shore of Loch
Brittle, and take the path down the east side of the
loch. After about 4 km the path runs inland,
crosses a substantial dyke and becomes less easy to
follow. It is probably easiest to stay close to the
lower edge of the hill on the right, walking
westwards on the south slope and gradually losing
height. Soon a loch should come into view, with a
short wall running from one end to the sea shore,
the cairn being just in front of the wall.

The chambered cairn of Rubh' an Dunain is not
conspicuous from a distance, being a low mound
largely covered with turf and heather, but it is a very
good example of a passage-grave of Hebridean type
and well worth the walk. The cairn is almost circular
on plan, measuring about 20 m in diameter and 3 m in
height, but on the south-east side the edge has been
recessed to form a concave forecourt with the entrance
passage at its centre. Several of the kerb-stones of the
forecourt remain in position, although some have now
fallen, and there are still traces of the drystone walling
that originally filled the gaps between the uprights.
The passage itself is nearly 3 m long and is still
lintelled. The outer lintel had slipped a little, but the

passage was obviously originally quite low and narrow at the outer end, becoming higher towards the chamber. There is a constriction in the side-walls nearly half-way in. The chamber, now roofless, is almost circular, and is walled by large upright slabs with drystone walling between.

Excavations in 1931 and 1932 showed that the cairn was built of rounded stones, probably from the beach nearby, and surrounded by a low wall of vertical slabs with walling between, similar to the interior. Pottery (including a Beaker), quartz pebbles, flint and quartz chips found in the excavations are in the RMS. The fragmentary remains of six adults of varying ages were found.

There are several other sites on the same point: 400 m to the south-east there is a small dun (NG 395159); also marked on the OS map there is a cave, excavation

of which in 1932 revealed Beaker pottery and a later iron forge with slag.

---

91 Unival, Chambered Cairn and Iron-Age House, North Uist.
3rd millennium BC for the cairn and later 1st millennium BC and early 1st millennium AD for the house.
NF 800668. Probably best approached from the Committee Road, which cuts North Uist from Sollas to Bayhead: leave the road before reaching the cattle grid at the south end and walk across the moor.

Several upright stones can be seen halfway down the profile of the hill. It is a complex monument with an earlier chambered tomb and the remains of a later iron-age house.

The cairn is low and square, some 16 m on each side. Some of the upright kerb-stones marking the edge still remain, with drystone walling between them, while others have now fallen. On the south-east side more remain and they increase in height towards the centre, where a short narrow passage leads into an irregularly shaped chamber of upright slabs measuring about 1.8 m by 2.2 m and now roofless. Excavation in 1935 and 1939 produced parts of the skeletons of two people from the chamber, and a large number of sherds from several different neolithic pots, a stone ball and a few pieces of worked flint and quartz.

There is a standing stone a short distance from the south-west corner of the cairn.

In the north-east corner of the cairn, an amorphous hollow is all that remains of an iron-age dwelling. The inhabitants apparently used the chamber itself as a cooking pit and large quantities of pottery were found in the house and in the chamber. The finds are now in RMS.

*Unival, Chambered Cairn, **North Uist** (no. 91).*

154

MUSEUMS

Several local museums have attractive displays about various aspects of the history and archaeology of Argyll and Bute, Lochaber and the Isles, as do museums in Edinburgh and Glasgow. We have not listed here castles with special displays, nor collections of sculptured slabs.

Auchindrain, Mid Argyll (no. 5), a working farming museum with an informative display on farming practices within the setting of the original buildings.

Bute Museum, Stuart Street, Rothesay, Bute. The museum of the Buteshire Natural History Society, built by the 4th Marquess of Bute in 1927, contains extensive archaeological and antiquarian collections, including several early crosses, quite apart from important natural history and geological exhibits. Finds from Rothesay Castle (no. 32) include a 10th or 11th century chess-man and several weapons.

Campbeltown Museum, Hall Street, Campbeltown, Kintyre; an interesting building (see no. 15) which contains a rich collection of prehistoric and later artefacts from Kintyre.

Easdale Island Folk Museum, Easdale Island, Lorn, has details of the slate workings on the island.

Royal Museum of Scotland, Queen Street, Edinburgh, holds many important finds from the west, including the objects from excavations in the

Kilmartin Valley and a cast of the Kildalton Cross (no. 45).

West Highland Museum, Cameron Square, Fort William. Displays of local archaeological and historical material.

Glasgow Art Gallery and Museum, Kelvingrove, Glasgow, has archaeological material from the west and a cast of the Kildalton Cross (no. 45).

Hunterian Museum, University of Glasgow, holds the finds from the important excavations of brochs at Dun Mor, Vaul, Tiree (no. 64) and Dun Ardtreck, Skye (no. 58), as well as an extensive range of prehistoric material.

Glencoe and North Lorn Folk Museum, Glen Coe, Lochaber; a small cruck-framed building with displays both of local history and of the slate industry.

Museum of Islay Life, Port Charlotte, Islay, contains a marvellous range of material outlining the prehistory and history of the island at all periods.

Arnol Blackhouse, Lewis (no. 4).

Shawbost School Museum, Shawbost, Lewis, includes displays relating to crofting, fishing and weaving.

Old Byre Heritage Centre, Dervaig, Mull; situated in Glen Bellart to the south-east of Dervaig, the museum describes crofting life on Mull.

Tobermory Museum, Mull, has objects and carved stones relating to the early history of the area.

McCaig Museum, Corran Halls, Oban, has a compact and interesting display of the growth of Oban and of local archaeological and historical objects.

The Clan Donald Centre at Armadale Castle, Skye (no. 1), contains information about the Clan and about one of its most famous members, Flora MacDonald; excellent audio-visual programme on Clan Donald history, particularly during the period of the Lordship of the Isles.

The Piping Centre, Borreraig, Skye, home of the famous MacCrimmon College of Piping; an exhibition in the Centre includes details of the structure of bagpipes, history of piping and famous piping families.

Three cottage museums in Skye, at Colbost (NG 216486), Kilmuir (NG 395718) and Luib (NG 565278), contain typical living rooms and a selection of agricultural implements and items used in fishing, weaving, and other industries.

On St. Kilda (no. 7) there is a small museum, open during the summer, with informative displays on the island's history.

South Uist Folk Museum, Eochar, South Uist; here a Hebridean thatched cottage contains displays illustrative of the crofting way of life of the southern Hebrides.

Museum nan Eilean, Steornabhagh, is situated in the former Town Hall of Stornoway (no. 18) and is the first of what is hoped will be a network of museums to serve the Western Isles; here there are attractive displays of the geology, archaeology and history of this part of Lewis.

EXCURSIONS

The excursions are intended to act as introductions to some of the more important island sites or mainland round trips; almost every route in the west has adjacent sites and in the course of a journey to some of our major monuments you will often discover unexpected examples of others, and we hope that our entries will give an impression of the date or context of such comparable sites. In such a personal assessment, we have chosen sites that we enjoy and tours that we know to be interesting. Almost all the sites we have included are shown on the relevant 1:50,000 map, along with many others; we hope that with the map and our guide, both the well-known sites and those on remoter hillsides will provide a focus for touring among some of the most beautiful of Scottish scenery. In mainland Argyll there are several good centres for excursions, though frequently the tour will be there and back on the same road; we offer two from which a selection of sites will have to be made depending on

timing. The monuments between the Crinan Canal and Kilmartin will probably occupy about a day in themselves. For those islands that are best explored on foot we have provided general descriptions of some of the more important sites rather than specific itineraries.

Canna

Canna is small, low and relatively flat, although it has some impressive cliffs. The major part of the island comprises one large farm, but there is a smaller tidal island, Sanday, on which there are several crofts most of which are still worked. Canna has probably always been more attractive to settlers than the adjacent island of Rum. The island formed part of the lands that belonged to the Benedictine monastery of Iona. There is a weathered cross, traditionally on the site of St Columba's chapel, north of the farm (NG 269055); the head and one arm of the cross are now missing; one face has a panel of key-pattern and a series of intertwined figures, the scenes on the other include reclining animals, a horseman, and possibly a figure intended to be a Virgin and Child. Sgor nam Ban-naomha, sometimes interpreted as an early Christian site, has a difficult descent, but may be seen from the cliffs above (NG 229043); here a strong wall encloses an area in which there are several smaller buildings one of which contains a well, whose water is channelled through another building on the east side

● Prehistoric & Roman
■ Castle
† Ecclesiastical
▲ Domestic
▲ Industrial
ʊ Miscellaneous

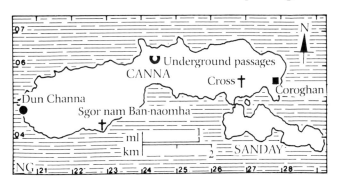

of the enclosure before dropping into the sea. This site is a very unusual one; the complex water-system defying easy interpretation, but it is possible that some of the buildings are bath-houses. Perhaps the waters were imbued with curative powers. Dun Channa (NG 205047), on a stack at the west end of the island, is also difficult of access, but is visible from the cliffs. Near the centre of the island are two short subterranean passages (NG 244062) with traces of structures, also of unknown date, in the vicinity. On the Coroghan (NG 279055) there is a small defensive structure approached by a hazardous path; this mortared keep with its timber lintel is probably of 17th century date or later.

Colonsay and Oronsay

The Oronsay excursion depends on the tides, for which take local advice; visit Oronsay Priory (no. 48), the iron-age fort 450 m to north-east Dun Domhnuill (NR 354890), and the mesolithic mounds in the dunes to the south of Seal Cottage (NR 358880).

On Colonsay itself the standing stones known as 'Fingal's Limpet Hammers', Lower Kilchattan, form an impressive pair (NR 367949); of the forts, Dun Cholla (NR 377915) and Dun Eibhinn (NR 382943) are both well-preserved, and the latter offers extensive views over the island; tiny duns are a feature of Colonsay, and the slight remains at Tobar Fuar (NR 357938), now the site of a tee on the golf-course, gives a good impression of the situation of many. The gardens of Colonsay House, Kiloran, are open (the house itself is an early 18th century mansion with many later additions); an unusual Early Christian cross-slab of about 8th century date has been sited beside a well dedicated to St Oran (NR 395968). The stone originally came from a burial ground at Riasg Buidhe 2 km to the south-east, and has a marvellously expressive portrait, possibly of a monk.

Islay

From Bowmore (no. 14) the excursion to the Rinns of Islay takes the A 846 to Bridgend; there take the left turn (A 847) towards Port Charlotte. Passing Islay House, the mansion house of the former proprietors of much of the island, the Campbells of Shawfield, the road skirts the head of Loch Indaal with an impressive standing stone on the right at Uiskentuie (NR 293633). Port Charlotte, a planned village begun in 1828, contains the Museum of Islay Life with excellent displays of the island's history and its present activities. In the playing-field to the south-west of the village is a chambered cairn of Clyde type (NR 248576). Continue south-west to Port Wemyss, with the lighthouse of

Orsay (no. 12) on the adjacent island, and to Portnahaven, where the church is a parliamentary kirk of T-plan (NR 169524). The road on the west side of the Rinns from Portnahaven to Port Charlotte passes the rather sorry stone circle at Cultoon (NR 195569) and the partly reconstructed later medieval chapel (NR 204601) and 19th century steading (NR 206603) at Kilchiaran; there are several carved stones including slabs of the Iona and Loch Sween schools in the chapel. From Port Charlotte continue north for 5 km and take the junction on the left to Kilchoman (NR 216632). Amid the sad setting of the abandoned church are several well-preserved grave-slabs and crosses, including two particularly fine later medieval

crosses of the Iona school. From Kilchoman continue north to Saligo and the Ballinaby standing stones (no. 75); skirt Loch Gorm before taking the B 8017, which passes through the extensive bronze-age settlement of An Sithean at NR 250665, turn north at Aoradh for 4.3 km to Kilnave (Cill Naoimh), where there is a worn but intricately carved Early Christian cross to the east of the ruined medieval chapel (NR 285715). From here return to Aoradh and continue to Bridgend and Bowmore.

Kintyre

Lochgilphead to Ardrishaig (A 83) to see the Crinan Canal basin (no. 10); continue to Tarbert Castle (no. 34); at Clachan/Seal View car park note the small dun of Ronachan Bay (NR 740548); the cairn of Corrichrevie is visible on the left at (NR 738540), continue to Killean (no. 46) and then pass the later parish church at A' Chleit (NR 681417). On to Campbeltown (no. 15) (the road on the east side of the peninsula is much slower). The dun at Kildonan is worth a visit (no 67); as are the stones and ruined monastery at Saddell (NR 784320). Carradale offers an impressive fort on Carradale Point (no. 53) for the active scrambler. Look out for a glimpse of Cour, a private house, on the east side of the road (NR 823481); this has been described as a 'wildly romantic house with battered chimneys and banks of round-headed mullion windows'. At Claonaig fork right to Skipness Castle (no. 33). Return via Tarbert, and the 19th century Stonefield Castle (NR 864717), to Lochgilphead.

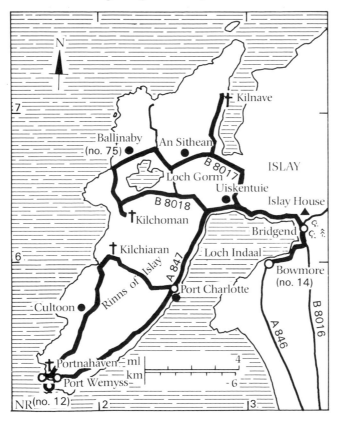

Lewis

Beginning in Stornoway (no. 18) on the A 858, after 5 km it is worth driving out along the Pentland Road (B 8012) to see some of the 'shielings' still used at peat cutting time and for holidays. There is a tremendous

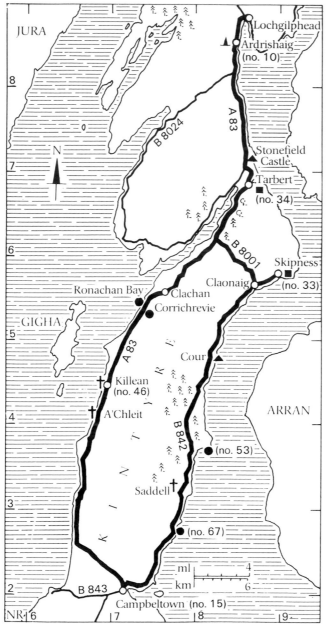

variety in these small seasonally occupied buildings. Return to the main road at Achmore (though the Pentland Road continues to Carloway, it is not suitable for cars on its central section), and continue to the standing stones at Callanish (no. 76). Then drive through Breascleit, noting the building formerly used for the accommodation of the Flannan Isles lightkeepers' families on the right, to the spectacular broch of Dun Carloway (no. 61). On the way to Shawbost, where there is a museum, there is a pleasant brief diversion in the form of a short walk along a marked path to a restored water mill at NB 244463, leaving the road at NB 244459.

Passing through Bragair, note the whalebone arch on the left, and the broch on an island in the loch on the right, and continue to Arnol Blackhouse (no. 4), before returning to Stornoway over the Barvas Moor.

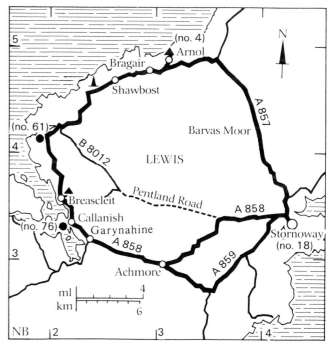

Oban to Dalmally and back

From Oban (no. 17) drive north to Dunbeg and
Dunstaffnage Castle (no. 25); pass below Connel
Bridge, noted for its huge cantilever span, and keeping
to the A 85, there is the possibility of visiting the
gardens of the Scots Baronial mansion of Achnacloich
(NM 955340); at Taynuilt fork left into the village
(noting the railway station) to Bonawe Furnace (no. 8).
To visit charcoal-burning platforms take the B 845 to
Glen Nant where the National Nature Reserve car park
(NN 019273) has details of a forest walk which
includes several platforms. Return to Taynuilt,
continue east on the A 85 to St Conan's Church, Loch
Awe (no. 2), Kilchurn Castle (no. 28) and Dalmally
Church (no. 38).

Return to Oban, possibly taking the minor road via
Glen Lonan which forks south at the Taynuilt Hotel,
and passes Diarmid's Pillar and cairn at Strontoiller
(no. 80).

Rum

Rum is one of the larger of the Hebrides, and is
dominated by the impressive hills known as the
Cuillin of Rum. The proportion of cultivable land is
small, and doubtless the population has never been
large. Rum is the only known source of bloodstone, an
attractive stone used in prehistoric times as an
alternative to flint; although there is evidence of
intensive manufacture of implements on the island,
and some have been found on Skye and the west coast,
there is no evidence of large-scale trade. In contrast to
its neighbour Skye, Rum has little evidence of
prehistoric settlement. Two crosses on stones at Bagh
na h-Uamha (NM 421973) and Kilmory (NG 361036)
and the placename Papadil suggest visits by Early
Christian monks.

The remains of some of the pre-clearance townships
may be seen at Bagh na h-Uamha (NM 420973),
Guirdil (NG 318011), Harris (NM 338959) and
Kilmory (NG 361036), and 19th century shepherds'
cottages are scattered over the island. These form an
interesting contrast with the squat grandeur of Kinloch
Castle (NM 401995), built in 1897 by Sir George

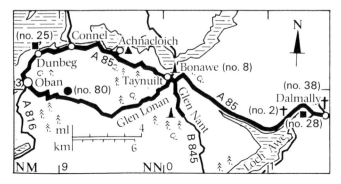

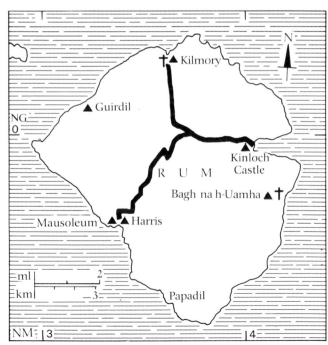

Bullough. A number of the rooms still contain the original furnishings. At Harris is the Bullough mausoleum (NM 336956), built in the style of a Greek temple, and, surprisingly perhaps, not incongruous in the Hebridean landscape. The number of shielings on the island is remarkable, for over 300 huts have been identified. Their age is not known, although all must be earlier than the 19th century clearance. Some are built on low mounds which suggest successive buildings and a long history of use. They were not necessarily all in use at the same time, and those of roughly rectangular shape may well be later than the more oval or rounded ones.

Skye

Beginning in Portree, go to Bracadale, seeing two carved grave-slabs in the churchyard (NG 355387) on the way to Dun Beag (no. 59). It is worth taking a detour on the Ullinish road opposite the dun to pass the remains of a chambered cairn just north of Ullinish Lodge (NG 323379) beside the road on the west side. Further along the road there are two impressive cairns at Vatten (NG 298439 and 297440). At Colbost there is a blackhouse museum, and here it is worth taking the turn marked Borreraig to go to the Piping Centre; instead of returning directly to Colbost, take the track to Glendale, to see a restored mill and an unusual carved stone in the graveyard (no. 41). Return to the main road and then go north to Dunvegan (nos 27 and 62). If there is time, an excursion along the Vatternish peninsula to see Trumpan Church and the brochs of Hallin, Borrafiach and Gearymore (no. 63) is worthwhile. On the way back to Portree, stop at Skeabost old bridge to see the ruined church with finely carved medieval effigies on the island just downstream (NG 418485), and the Pictish symbol stone at Tote (no. 52). At Borve there is a linear setting of standing stones close to the village loop-road (NG 451480).

BIBLIOGRAPHY

Argyll and Bute District Council, *Argyll and Bute tourist planning map and gazetteer*, Edinburgh, 1983.

Bannerman, J W M 'The Lordship of the Isles', in *Scottish Society in the Fifteenth Century*, Brown, J M (ed), 209-40, London, 1977.

Cameron, A D *Getting to know . . . the Crinan Canal*, Edinburgh, 1978.

Cruden, S *The Scottish Castle*, Edinburgh, 1960.

Dunbar, J G *The Historic Architecture of Scotland*, London, 1966; revised edition, 1978.

Dunbar, J G and Fisher, I *Iona*, Edinburgh, 1983.

Dunlop, J *The British Fisheries Society 1786-1893*, Edinburgh, 1978.

Fenton, A *The Island Blackhouse and a guide to 'The Blackhouse'*, *No. 42*, *Arnol*, Edinburgh, 1978.

Fenton, A *A Farming Township; Auchindrain, Argyll*, Perth, 1979.

Hay, G D and Stell, G P *Bonawe Iron Furnace*, Edinburgh, 1984.

Henshall, A S *The Chambered Tombs of Scotland*, Edinburgh, 1963, and 1972.

Lindsay, I G and Cosh, M *Inveraray and the Dukes of Argyll*, Edinburgh, 1973.

Lindsay, J *The Canals of Scotland*, Newton Abbot, 1968.

MacKie, E W *Dun Mor Vaul: an iron-age broch on Tiree*, Glasgow, 1974.

MacKie, E W *Scotland: an Archaeological Guide*, London, 1975.

MacLean, L (ed) *The Middle Ages in the Highlands*, Inverness, 1981; including Munro, J 'The Lordship of the Isles', 23-37; Dunbar, J G 'The medieval architecture of the Scottish Highlands', 38-70.

McNeill, P and Nicholson, R (eds) *An historical atlas of Scotland, c. 400—c. 1600*, St Andrews, 1975; second edition, 1980.

Munro, R W *Scottish Lighthouses*, Stornoway, 1979.

Murray, W H *The islands of Western Scotland*, London, 1973.

Piggott, S *Scotland before history*, Edinburgh, 1982; with a gazetteer of ancient monuments by G Ritchie.

Ritchie, A *Scotland BC*, Edinburgh, 1988.

Ritchie, G and Ritchie, A *Scotland: Archaeology and Early History*, London, 1981.

Ritchie, J N G *Brochs of Scotland*, Aylesbury, 1988.

Royal Commission on the Ancient and Historical Monuments of Scotland *An Inventory of the Ancient Monuments and Constructions in the Outer Hebrides, Skye and the Small Isles*, Edinburgh, 1928.

Royal Commission on the Ancient and Historical Monuments of Scotland *Argyll: an Inventory of the Monuments*; vol. 1, Kintyre, 1971; vol. 2, Lorn, 1975; vol. 3, Mull, Tiree, Coll and Northern Argyll, 1980;

vol. 4, Iona, 1982; vol. 5, Islay, Jura, Colonsay and Oronsay, 1984; vol. 6, Mid Argyll and Cowal:

Prehistoric and Early Historic Monuments, 1988; vol. 7, Mid Argyll and Cowal: Medieval and Later Monuments, forthcoming.

Small, A (ed) *A St Kilda Handbook*, Edinburgh, 1979.

Smout, T C *A History of the Scottish People, 1560-1830*, London, 1969.

Steer, K A and Bannerman, J W M *Late Medieval Monumental Sculpture in the West Highlands*, Edinburgh, 1977.

Stell, G P and Harman, M *Buildings of St Kilda*, Edinburgh, 1988.

Taylor, W *The Military Roads in Scotland*, Newton Abbot, 1976.

Thomson, D S (ed) *The Companion to Gaelic Scotland*, Oxford, 1983.

Whittow, J B *Geology and Scenery in Scotland*, London, 1977.

INDEX

Printed in Scotland for HMSO by (25801)
Dd. 287375   H/F4379   C70   3/90